CONCILIUM

THEOLOGY IN THE AGE OF RENEWAL

CONCILIUM

CONCILIUM/VOL. 21

DOGMA

MAN
AS
MAN & BELIEVER

Volume 21

CONCILIUM
theology in the age of renewal

PAULIST PRESS
NEW YORK, N.Y. / GLEN ROCK, N.J.

Library of Congress Catalogue Card Number: 67-17789

Suggested Decimal Classification: 232

Paulist Press assumes responsibility for the accuracy of the English translations in this Volume.

PAULIST PRESS
EXECUTIVE OFFICES: 304 W. 58th Street, New York, N.Y. and 21 Harris-
    town Road, Glen Rock, N.J.
Executive Publisher: John A. Carr, C.S.P.
Executive Manager: Alvin A. Illig, C.S.P.
Asst. Executive Manager: Thomas E. Comber, C.S.P.

EDITORIAL OFFICES: 304 W. 58th Street, New York, N.Y.
Editor: Kevin A. Lynch, C.S.P.
Managing Editor: Urban P. Intondi

Printed and bound in the United States of America by
The Colonial Press Inc., Clinton, Mass.

CONTENTS

ix

PREFACE

Edward Schillebeeckx, O.P./*Nijmegen, Netherlands*
Boniface Willems, O.P./*Nijmegen, Netherlands*

The necessary renewal of theology has already made clear progress in many and various sectors. However, it is gradually becoming more and more manifest that parts of this renewal imply a central problem. An earlier generation might have called this the problem of the nature of Christianity. This problem is indeed the key issue even now, but it is becoming more sharply defined. Every branch of theology has already felt the far-reaching changes that are taking place, particularly in the fields of anthropology and epistemology. For all the faithful, the basic issue arising from all this is the question: What is the relation between man as man and man as believer? And this obviously leads to questions about revelation, faith, dogma and the magisterium or the teaching function of the Church.

This set of problems broke through again and again in the discussions on the *Dogmatic Constitution on Divine Revelation* at Vatican Council II. The laborious manner in which the final text of this Constitution was finally achieved showed how basic the questions at stake were. This was also apparent in the fact that the World Council of Churches at Montreal, 1963, was confonted with similar problems (van Leeuwen).

The increase in secularization and the realization of the legitimacy of this process ultimately force Christians to confront the dilemma whether revelation is a divine speaking "from outside" or the expression and enlightenment of man's self-understanding. Possibly this is not really a dilemma because God and man are not "competitors" on the same level (Bakker).

Every preacher is faced with the task of making the unique revelation of Christ relevant at all times. Therefore, his explanation of the Gospel has to present the historically conditioned ways of expressing Christ's message in a new kerygmatic form. The one and only historical revelation must become accessible to all. This phenomenon already operates within scripture itself (Vögtle).

The shades of meaning that can be found in the concept of revelation obviously lead to shades of meaning in man's responsive attitude toward it: i.e., faith. Man's believing response to God has a definite kind of content precisely because of God's revelation in and through Christ's incarnation (Alfaro).

Occasionally the Church's magisterium has given this content a binding expression in dogmas. But what held for scripture itself also holds for these dogmas: they must be preached in a way that is relevant. This will be of great importance when we reflect on the infallibility of this dogma-declaring magisterium (Baum).

We also ought to realize that a *truth* of faith, such as it appears in scripture, is not quite the same as what today is generally meant by a "truth". A truth of *faith* demands of man a total and existential commitment (von Balthasar). Therefore, the science of theology has a character peculiarly its own. In particular, the theologian should remain aware of the fact that his function is to serve a community of faith, the Church (Chenu).

The various opinions about the development of dogma among Catholic (Hammans) and Protestant (Lindbeck) theologians are given in the Bibliographical Survey. A documentary contribution shows how far back we can trace the "traditional" meaning of the word "dogma" in history (Kasper). A brief report on the international theological Congress (Rome, October, 1966), which dealt with the theology of Vatican Council II, concludes this volume of *Concilium*.

PART I
ARTICLES

Peter van Leeuwen, O.F.M. / *Alverna, Netherlands*

The Dogmatic Constitution on Divine Revelation

The Original Plan

It was the original intention to place before the Council two schemas for dogmatic constitutions. One proposed how to preserve integrally the deposit of faith, and under this title a number of tenets of the faith that were said to be in danger were put together, including, among others, the idea of truth, public revelation and the Catholic faith. The other dealt with the Church and formed the central theme of the Council at its inception. Originally, scripture and tradition were part of this second schema and appeared in the chapter on the magisterium which is entrusted with the custody, protection and explanation of the faith contained in these two sources.[1] However, this section on scripture and tradition soon developed into a schema of its own because its content became too vast to become a subsection of the schema on the Church and also because Pope John demanded special attention for this topic.[2] Thus, the schema on

---

[1] Report of the first plenary session of the preparatory theological commission (October 27, 1960).

[2] Cf. the aforementioned report: "But since the supreme pontiff insisted so strongly on the question of the sources that was first put into the schema on the Church, it was considered better to separate this question of the sources from that of the Church because otherwise it would occupy a disproportionately large place in the schema on the Church." A decision was also made to divide the schema on the integral preservation of the deposit into one on "matters of faith" and one on "matters

the sources of revelation became the first in a series of dogmatic schemas, while revelation itself remained part of the schema on the deposit of faith. This latter schema was never considered by the Council, but was quietly allowed to slip out of the agenda after the schema on the sources had been assigned by the pope to a mixed commission for revision in November, 1962.

The Schemas of 1962

In a certain sense, those who were charged with these schemas stuck loyally to the task set for them by the pope, namely, working out the wishes and directives of the Council fathers and Roman Congregations which had been compiled by the "ante-preparatory" commission. Scripture and tradition formed an important part of these *desiderata*. A number of bishops demanded clear pronouncements on the inspiration and inerrancy of scripture, on modern exegesis in connection with literary *genres* and, in particular, on the historicity of the gospels. Attention was also demanded for that current of thought claiming tradition to be more an explanation of scripture rather than an addition to its contents. Certain bishops asked for a statement that tradition was a second source, complementing the content of scripture.

of morals". When the preparatory commissions were set up on June 5, 1960, only the theological commission had been given a more concrete description of its function: namely, that it should consider and thoroughly investigate the questions that pertain to holy scripture, sacred tradition, faith and morals: (*A.A.S.* [1960], p. 435; *Acta et documenta Concilio Oecumenico Vaticano II apparando*, Series I [antepraeparatoria], Vol. I: *Acta Summi Pontificis Ioannis XXIII* [Rome, 1960], p. 94).

In an audience given to the general secretary of the central preparatory commission on July 2, 1960, the pope asked the theological commission to deal with the following questions, among others, though he left them free to add others: (1) the sources of revelation, setting forth, according to statements made by recent popes, the Catholic doctrine on holy scripture (i.e., the historicity of the sacred writings and the obedience due to sacred tradition and the Church's magisterium by biblical scholars); (2) errors to be condemned on this question while laying down suitable norms by which such scholars may be led in their interpretation of the sacred writings according to the mind of the Church" (cf. *Pontificia commissio centralis praeparatoria Concilii Vaticani II. Quaestiones commissionibus praeparatoriis Concilii Vaticani II positae*, p. 7).

The use of scripture, particularly in modern translations, was also included in the bishops' demands.[3] These demands lay at the origin of this schema: the first chapter on the twofold source of revelation, followed by four chapters on scripture, one on the inspiration, inerrancy and explanation of scripture, one on the Old Testament, one on the New Testament and one on scripture in the Church.

The schema "on the integral preservation of the deposit of faith" was mainly inspired by the "proposals and exhortations" of the Holy Office and of the Congregation on Seminaries and Universities. Their first intention was directed against the still-present threats of rationalism, modernism and immanentism. Therefore, they wanted to have the unchangeable Catholic teaching confirmed on the knowledge of truth, the knowledge of God, creation and evolution, public revelation and Catholic faith, development of doctrine, private revelations, the natural and supernatural orders, original sin, the four last things and Christ's atonement, and to have the relevant errors condemned.[4]

The teaching on revelation in this second schema can briefly be summarized. Public revelation is the divine communication of the mysteries of salvation and the truths connected thereto. Although this revelation is given to us in the history of salvation, it is not restricted to this history. The events of salvation are revelation only because of the teaching contained in them, but this teaching also contains general truths, particularly the mystery of God himself and of the divine Persons. Revelation is identical with revealed teaching and as such is the object of faith. This revelation reaches its fullness in Christ because he

[3] *Acta et documenta*, Series I, Vol. II: *Consilia et vota Episcoporum et Praelatorum* (Rome, 1961). This comprises ten volumes, of which two form an appendix with an analytical table. Cf. especially, pp. 16 and 32. In this preparatory phase most of the warnings apparently came from the bishops!

[4] *Acta et documenta*, Series I, Vol. III: *Proposita et monita SS. Congregationum Curiae Romanae* (Rome, 1960), pp. 4 and 316. Cf. also the *Votum Supremae S. Congregationis Sancti Officii* for the theological commission, where it is said that all the errors condemned by Vatican Council I "are alive again today and threaten to radically undermine the faith and the whole Christian religion".

has proclaimed to us the perfect teaching of revelation. That formulations and concepts in which this revealed teaching is expressed should be seen as proximate, always open to improvement and modification—either because of a deeper understanding of the mystery or because of changes in our habits of thought —is something to be condemned as a new and dangerous relativism.[5]

This was the foundation of the doctrine of the two sources, expressed in the solemn declaration: "Holy Mother Church has always believed and believes that the fullness of revelation is not contained exclusively in scripture, but in scripture and tradition as in a double source, though in different ways." Scripture is a God-given aid for the expression and explanation of the truths of faith. Its meaning, however, can only be known fully and with certainty through tradition. "Tradition, indeed, and this alone, is the way by which the Church can clearly know a number of revealed truths, particularly those that refer to the inspiration, canonicity and integrity of all books together and of each book in particular." God has entrusted the task of preserving these two sources of revelation as one treasury of the faith, and of providing the authentic interpretation thereof, not to individual believers, however learned, but only to the living magisterium of the Church. This is therefore the general and the proximate rule of faith. By this rule, the content of the two sources of revelation is explained, and what is obscurely or implicitly contained in this is unfolded.[6]

Rejection of the Schema on the Two Sources of Revelation

This schema of 1962 was rejected mainly for two reasons. First of all, this text did not correspond to the purpose of the

---

[5] "Schema constitutionis dogmaticae de deposito fidei pure custodiendo," in *Schemata constitutionum et decretorum de quibus disceptabitur in Concilii sessionibus*, Series I (Rome, 1962), Ch. IV, "De revelatione publica et de fide catholica," pp. 36-38.

[6] "Schema constitutionis dogmaticae de Fontibus Revelationis," in *Schemata*, Series I, Ch. I, "De duplici fonte Revelationis," pp. 9-11.

Council as it had been declared by Pope John, especially in his opening address—namely, not to concentrate on particular dogmas but rather on a contemporary presentation of Catholic doctrine as a whole in a way that might promote union among Christians. The schema was neither pastoral nor ecumenical. The text was also rejected because, without any compelling reasons, it cast suspicion on particular opinions of theologians and exegetes of sound reputation and hampered their work. This also applied to what the fourth chapter said about the historicity of the gospels.[7]

The Schema of 1963

The result of the work of the mixed commission, composed of the doctrinal commission, the Secretariat for Promoting Christian Unity and some cardinals, was put before the Council fathers in April, 1963, but showed only little progress. Following Trent, only one source is mentioned: namely, the Gospel. There is no longer any mention of a number of revealed truths that would only be found in tradition. The question of the historicity of the gospels was formulated differently. However, the text remained stranded in an equivocal notion about revelation and in a too vague definition of tradition and its relation to scripture.[8] It was too obviously a compromise, and as such produced a certain satisfaction at the elimination of offensive points, but

[7] This formulation is obviously a simplification of all kinds of observations, made either orally during the debate on this schema or in writing. An analysis of these observations would give a far more varied picture, particularly with regard to the terms "pastoral" and "ecumenical" which from here on begin to play an important part in the Council, but continue to suffer from a certain vagueness and ambiguity. The pope's address is repeatedly quoted in these emendations (cf. *A.A.S.* 54 [1962], pp. 786ff.). The most important aspects were: (1) the need to proclaim Catholic teaching in accordance with this modern age; (2) the treatment not of specific dogmas, but rather of Catholic teaching as a whole, according to the method that suits our times; (3) the distinction between the unchangeable truth in itself and its formulation in a way corresponding to modern demands.

[8] *Schema constitutionis dogmaticae de divina revelatione* (1963).

there was also some constructive criticism, particularly with regard to revelation and its transmission.[9]

The Final Text

The coordination commission, therefore, asked the doctrinal
commission on January 3, 1964, once again to revise the schema
that had not been debated in Council. Thus, in July, 1964, they
presented to the conciliar fathers a text that was greatly modified, particularly with regard to the chapters on revelation itself,
its transmission and scripture in the Church. This schema became
the basis of the Constitution.[10]

With special reference to 1 John 1, 2-3, the content was now
described as the authentic doctrine of divine revelation and its
transmission (n. 1). A separate chapter was devoted to revelation itself. The earlier chapter on public revelation in the schema
on the integral preservation of the deposit of faith now came
first, but it was completely reshaped.

God Reveals Himself

"It has pleased God in his goodness and wisdom to reveal himself, and to make known the secret hidden in his will" (n. 2).
The text thus begins with this definition of revelation, taken over
from Vatican Council I (Denz. 3004 [1785]) without any previous mention of a natural revelation.

This revelation in which God invites man to communion with
him is realized in deeds and words so closely interconnected that
the deeds reinforce the words and the words proclaim and cast

[9] *Patrum conciliarium animadversiones de divina revelatione, inde a
die 10m. Iunii 1963* (stencilled).
[10] *Schema constitutionis de divina revelatione* (1964). The qualification
"dogmaticae" was omitted here, as in the schema on the Church, through
some unknown but not accidental cause. This was changed at the demand
of the majority in the commission.

light upon God's deeds (n. 2). The accompanying report (*relatio*) of this text calls revelation historical and sacramental: "historical because it consists first of all in everything where God intervenes . . . sacramental because the full meaning of the deeds can only be known to us through the words—that is, through God's speaking, which is itself an historical event".[11] Through this revelation the profound truth concerning God and human salvation shines for us in Christ (n. 2).

The prophetic character of the Word—which not only casts light on God's deeds but which, above all, places human existence and the whole of history under the judgment, the promise and the blessing of God's Word—is insufficiently elaborated; indeed, it is hardly mentioned at all. In this text the Word is still too limited to an explanatory function.

This definition of divine revelation as salvation history puts Christ at the center as the one who fulfills it by the total fact of his presence and his public declaration of himself, by words and deeds through which he completed his salvific mission, especially through his death and glorious resurrection, and, finally, by sending the Spirit of truth. In and through him God is always with us to deliver us from the darkness of sin and death and to raise us again to eternal life (n. 4).

Thus it is Christ who, from beginning to end, determines the history of mankind. In the order of actual fact there is therefore no room for a so-called natural revelation as an autonomous phase or as a factual possibility. The witness that God bears to himself in creatures (Rom. 1, 19f.) is linked with the Word through whom all has been created (Jn. 1, 3), and is contained in that saving revelation through which God made himself known to our first parents from the beginning. This preparation for the Gospel embraces the whole of history and all peoples and is in no way eliminated through sin, for, after man's fall, God again raised him by his promise of redemption to hope in salvation (n. 3).

---

[11] *Relatio super cap. I et cap. II schematis constitutionis de divina revelatione* (1964).

This statement implies an appreciation of the value of religious life beyond the boundaries of the Old and New Testaments on the basis of God's universal revelation. This, in turn, provided the basis for the conciliar *Declaration on Non-Christian Religions*. It seems reasonable not to consider this preparation for the Gospel as limited to the period before Christ, but as extending to the whole of mankind insofar as it has not yet reached Christ explicitly.

To this preparation belong the call of Abraham and God's revelation to Israel as explicit revelation. Does this not underrate the Old Testament? The fourth chapter indeed mentions the lasting significance of the Old Testament for Christians and the unity of both Testaments. But even this still seems to limit it too much to the preparatory aspect. This limitation may also explain how Israel came to be mentioned in the context of the conciliar *Declaration on Non-Christian Religions*.

After the sections on revelation there follows a brief description of the faith, mainly filled with quotations from Vatican Council I and the Second Council of Orange. New in this text is the statement that man abandons himself freely and entirely to God in faith, and that the Holy Spirit, who moves man toward this faith, unceasingly perfects it by his gifts in order that his understanding of revelation may become more profound (n. 5). These words already ring in the growth of tradition. For the rest it is clear that so much attention was given to revelation itself and its transmission that faith was only mentioned in passing, as it were.

The last section (n. 6) of this chapter, unofficially titled "The Revealed Truths", seems to contain an undeveloped and almost alien element. It first mentions the natural knowability of God, already mentioned in the third section as God's witness in creatures, and then the indispensability of revelation for some truths not in themselves inaccessible to human reason. That this has not been properly worked out may be concluded from the fact that this particular section was practically left unmodified. In 1962 it appeared in the first chapter of the schema on the integral preservation of the deposit of faith. In 1963 it was placed at the end of the chapter on revelation under the title of "Natural Truths Connected with Revelation". By giving a literal quotation of Vatican Council I it was possible to avoid any discussion on this point, although there it was organically linked with natural revelation, the moral necessity of supernatural revelation for specific natural truths and the strict necessity of the revelation of the mysteries of salvation in the general purpose of the supernatural order. No attempt was even made to clarify the connection of this last section with the concept of revelation as expressed in the first sections.

The Orthodox Churches objected to this first chapter in that it did not take sufficient account of the Trinity. Too little was said about the revelation of the Holy Spirit. It was not made sufficiently clear that the Holy Spirit forms the historic Church and so makes Christ's resurrection the axis of history and leads the Church to the full truth.[12] This activity of the Spirit forms the community and determines history. In this way this activity completes the revelation of the Trinity which remains the foundation of the Church. In the opinion of the Orthodox Churches, this point was not adequately handled.

Another fact may be connected with this. The text mentions only incidentally and briefly the final revelation of Jesus Christ, in the sense that, after God's revelation in Christ, no further public revelation is to be expected until the glorious manifestation of our Lord Jesus Christ (n. 4). However, in scripture this seems to be the fullness of revelation toward which the Spirit leads us.[13]

The Transmission of Divine Revelation

The transmission of revelation, which occupied only a modest place in the schema of 1962,[14] has now become the central and

[12] Nikos A. Nissiotis, "Report on the Second Vatican Council," in The Ecumenical Review 18 (1966), p. 193.
[13] Cf. 1 Jn. 2, 28; 1 Pet. 1, 13; 5, 4; Lk. 17, 30; 1 Cor. 1, 7. There is perhaps inadequate treatment of the historical happening, the present and the future of revelation.
[14] Schema const. dogm. de font. rev. (1962), Ch. I, n. 3: "De trans-

all-embracing theme of the Constitution, together with revelation itself. The enduring foundation of this transmission is the mission of Christ and the sending of the Spirit. It therefore embraces both the apostolic and the post-apostolic transmission of revelation, and these two phases are so intimately connected that the Church will always find its definition and norm in its apostolic origin. The scriptures are placed within this transmission of revelation by the teaching, example and institutions of the apostles. Therefore, scripture cannot validly be separated from this transmission of revelation, for it is an essential part of it (n. 7).

And yet, in the sections that follow, scripture and tradition are mentioned again as two separate things; further on, tradition, scripture and the ecclesiastical magisterium are classed as three distinct entities. This seems to have been the result of preoccupation with the Reformation controversy.

In this document tradition appears for the first time before scripture. The texts of 1962 and 1963 still spoke of scripture and tradition in such a way that tradition could easily be understood as an addition to the content of the scriptures. In the texts of 1964 and 1965 tradition is deliberately placed first.

The meaning of this change is not merely that tradition preceded scripture but rather that tradition is more comprehensive and in fact includes scripture. "By means of this same tradition the complete canon of the sacred books becomes known to the Church, and the sacred letters themselves are more profoundly understood and made indefectibly contemporary in it." Tradition embraces all that "the apostles have transmitted and everything that leads to the sanctification of the life of the People of God and to the growth of faith". In this tradition "the Church, in its doctrine, life and worship perpetuates and transmits to all generations all that it is and all that it believes" (n. 8). Tradition is therefore total and is expressed in many ways. Within this tradition, scripture occupies the very special place due to the liv-

---

missione revelationis Novi Foederis." This follows here after the "first diffusion" by the apostles (n. 2).

ing Word of God, written down once and for all as the fixed preaching of the apostles, and for this reason stands above, and dominates, the Church and its tradition.

This first place given to tradition makes it clear that scripture belongs to it, although in a very special way. However, the wider comprehensiveness of tradition does not mean that tradition adds to scripture, even insofar as the strictly dogmatic content of faith is concerned. There is hardly any further basis for this opinion in the teaching on revelation and its transmission as presented in this Constitution.

Another new element stands out particularly when we compare this Constitution with Trent and Vatican Council I: tradition is no longer described as the embodiment of the unchangeable but as growth. "This tradition that issues from the apostles progresses in the Church under the assistance of the Holy Spirit. Insight into the realities and the words grows: this results from contemplation and study by the faithful who ponder them in their heart, from their experience of a profound understanding of spiritual realities, from the preaching of those who, with the episcopal succession, received the unfailing charism of the truth" (n. 8). Tradition and development are so intimately related to one another that we must say that not only our knowledge of tradition develops, but also tradition itself.[15] And here we certainly should not think primarily of the so-called development of dogma by way of deduction, but rather of the always contemporary nature of tradition that is indeed defined as transmitting divine revelation and making it operative in the historical present.

Nothing now remains to identify tradition with the magisterium. However, within tradition the magisterium still has the special function of authoritative judging and guiding in the truth in an authentic way—i.e., with official authority, in union with the whole People of God, and not standing above the Word of God, but rather serving it (n. 10).

Two questions arise at this point. First of all, there is the

[15] *Relatio prior de modibus a patribus propositis et a commissione doctrinali expensis, circa proemium et duo priora capita* (Oct. 22, 1965).

question of one tradition as opposed to many and various traditions. The Constitution only speaks of tradition in the singular,
except where it refers to 2 Thessalonians 2, 15 (n. 8). In this
the document differs from those of earlier councils: the Second
Council of Nicaea (787), which mentions both the one tradition of the Catholic Church and the concrete traditions; the
Council of Constantinople (870), which links up with this; the
Council of Trent, which mentions apostolic traditions in the
plural; Vatican Council I, which repeats the tridentine formula
and adds the formula of the written or transmitted Word of
God.[16] By this exclusive mention of tradition in the singular the
Constitution also differs most clearly from the report of the
Montreal Conference on tradition and traditions, which asks
precisely by what criterion the many traditions can be checked
against the one tradition.[17]

The Constitution does not identify tradition with the historical Church and all its traditions, of whatever kind. This is obvious from the limitation "which comes from the apostles", and
"which leads to the sanctification of the life of the People of
God and to the growth of faith". The words, "And so the Church
perpetuates and transmits . . . all that it is" (n. 8), must therefore be understood as meaning all that it is in truth, as the
Church of faith. In the same way it would be wrong to connect
this name of genuine tradition to every random development on
the ground that tradition is linked with growth: this can only
apply to a development in which the Church genuinely strives
"after the fullness of divine truth" (n. 8).

How then do we distinguish tradition from traditions, as the
Montreal Report asks? The Constitution places first the unanimity "of all the holy people, together with its pastors", and then
the authentic interpretation of the Word of God, whether scrip-

---

[16] *Conciliorum Oecumenicorum decreta* (Freiburg im Br., 1962), pp.
109f., 142f., 639, 781ff.; *Denz.-Sch.*, nn. 600f. (302f.), 650f. (336f.),
1501 (783), 3000f. (1781f.).

[17] *The Fourth World Conference on Faith and Order. The Report from
Montreal, 1963*, ed. by P. C. Rodger and L. Vischer (London, 1963):
Section II: "Scripture, Tradition and Traditions," pp. 50f.

tural or traditional, through the living voice of the Church's magisterium (n. 10). It is only in union with the whole community of the faithful that the magisterium can exercise its salutary function, not as "above God's Word" but as serving it and "teaching only what has been transmitted" (n. 10).

In answering the question of how to distinguish traditions from tradition, the Montreal Report rather sharply contrasts the Orthodox and Catholic positions. According to this Report the Orthodox would see the criterion in the whole community of the faithful, the Catholics exclusively in the magisterium. This seems incorrect.[18]

A second question, constantly and insistently asked by the Reformation, is whether in this Catholic doctrine the whole Church—particularly the ecclesiastical magisterium—remains clearly enough subject and obedient to holy scripture. Is it clear enough here that scripture stands "over against" or "vis-à-vis" the Church as a whole, and particularly the magisterium, so that the Church listens to it obediently, and is constantly led and renewed by it?[19]

The Reformed Churches seem to find it difficult to reconcile a magisterium that is subject to God's Word with a magisterium that can pronounce an authentic judgment. The Orthodox have less difficulty with this. They recognize "that in the text the magisterium is never thought of as an authority superior to scripture and tradition, but only in absolute union and agreement with them". Furthermore, the Eastern tradition possesses a unique feature in that it limits authority and magisterium to confirmation by the Church as a whole.[20]

Not until the last chapter on scripture in the life of the Church does the Constitution seem to work itself free from the controversy between Rome and the Reformation and to speak more freely in a genuine ecumenical and pastoral spirit. This is the chapter that the Protestant side has most widely appreciated.

[18] Ibid., p. 53.
[19] Lukas Vischer, "After the Fourth Session of the Second Vatican Council," in The Ecumenical Review 18 (1966), p. 156.
[20] Nikos A. Nissiotis, op. cit., p. 192.

The Church venerates the sacred scriptures even as it venerates the body of Christ; it accepts these scriptures, together with
tradition, as the supreme rule of its faith. "All the Church's
preaching, therefore, like the Christian religion itself, must feed
on, and be ruled by, holy scripture" (n. 21). The 1964 text
used "must be judged" (*iudicatur*). However, some fathers
thought this expression was too sharp and in the revised text it
was replaced by the less meaningful "feed on" (*nutritur*); finally,
the stronger term "ruled" (*regitur*) was added. Scripture is
then called the living Word of God, the Church's support and
source of energy, and for its children the kernel of their faith
(n. 21), the soul of theology (n. 24), a lasting force of strength
and renewal.

The Ecumenical Perspective

Together with the report on tradition and traditions, discussed
and accepted by the World Council of Churches in its Conference on Faith and Order in 1963, the Constitution has poured
new hope and a fresh stimulus into the dialogue precisely on
this difficult point that has divided the Churches. The authority
of the two documents obviously differs. The Montreal Report
was only briefly discussed in the Assembly and only has representative value insofar as it is actually accepted and operative.
But the conciliar text, although much more representative and
authoritative, should not be considered to be the last word on
the matter, but rather to bear witness to that growth of tradition of which the text itself speaks. There is now profound agreement on the concept of revelation itself and on the principle of
its transmission. The Montreal Report also puts tradition before
scripture.[21] The remaining questions, which can only now be

[21] *The Report from Montreal, 1963, op. cit.,* p. 51: "In our present
situation we wish to consider the problem of scripture and tradition, or
rather that of tradition and scripture. Therefore we wish to propose the
following statement as a fruitful way of reformulating the question. Our
starting point is that we are all living in a tradition that goes back to our

fruitfully posed, concern, above all, the dominion of God's Word over the Church, the distinction between tradition, traditions and the function of the magisterium, and particularly the pope's pastoral function within the function of the episcopal college and the whole community of the faithful.

Lord and has its roots in the Old Testament, and we are all indebted to that tradition inasmuch as we have received the revealed truth, the Gospel, through its being transmitted from one generation to another. Thus we can say that we exist as Christians by the tradition of the Gospel (the paradosis of the kerygma) testified to in scripture and transmitted in and by the Church through the power of the Holy Spirit. Tradition taken in this sense is actualized in the preaching of the Word, in the administration of the sacraments and worship, in Christian teaching and theology, and in mission and witness to Christ by the lives of the members of the Church." This declaration is followed by the distinction between traditions and tradition and the delineation of these two terms.

Leo Bakker, S.J. / *Maastricht, Netherlands*

What Is Man's Place in Divine Revelation?

Revelation has become a dominant theme not only in Protestant theology but also increasingly in Catholic theology, provoking innumerable questions. Here I wish to concentrate only on one basic question: Is revelation a speaking by God that falls vertically on man, as it were, from outside and without any contribution from man himself, or may revelation be taken as expressing and enlightening man's understanding of himself? In the first part of this article I will present a survey of how the problem developed, while in the second I will offer some further reflections on this problem.

I

THE PROBLEM AS IT STANDS TODAY

1. *The Problem in Itself*

Some ten years ago the Netherlands Humanist Association (*Nederlands Humanistisch Verbond*—*not* theistic) drafted a new declaration of principles stating that the humanist philosophy of life is "characterized by the attempt to understand life and the world with the help of the human faculties and *without starting from a particular revelation*". In an earlier declaration this last phrase was changed to read, "without starting from the existence of a personal deity". The change expressed in the new declaration thus brought a sharper and better formulation of its opposition to the Christian concept of life. The difficulty was no longer so much with faith in a personal God as with faith in a personal God who reveals.

Shortly afterward, H. Bonger, a member of this association, gave the following commentary on this statement: "Humanism cannot accept any other valid source of knowledge than that contained in the life of man's own spirit. The humanist does not start from a particular revelation, such as given in the bible or the Church's tradition, for the simple reason that he has no inner experience of it." [1]

With these words Bonger undoubtedly formulated the objection that has turned many of our contemporaries, in Holland as in other countries, against any revealed religion and has made them abandon Christianity. They do not primarily object to the existence of God or even to revelation in itself, but to a revelation that can neither be controlled nor verified and yet claims to be the guiding principle of human life. They consider themselves to be faced with the dilemma of a life guided by revelation *or* a life guided by experience. In this dilemma they have resolutely opted for experience.

It would be easy to compose an international anthology of all kinds of books and witnesses, provided by people who are no longer Christians, containing statements expressing the same views as those of the Dutch humanists. To give only one example, the German humanist C. Szczesny wrote: "The history of the difficult struggle between Christian dogma and the conclusions of modern science shows in an impressive manner the inevitable defeat of a spiritual outlook that wants to maintain, by hook or by crook, all kinds of positions already wrenched by experience from this spiritual philosophy. The Church's condemnation of the Copernican theory at the trial of Galileo in 1616 was only

---

[1] H. Bonger, "Modern Humanisme," in *Modern niet-godsdienstig humanisme*, p. 32.

withdrawn in 1835. But is was withdrawn. As soon as a presentation of the faith conflicts with facts of experience, it loses more and more of its persuasive power until, finally, it descends to the level of mere literature." [2]

However, not only those who are no longer Christians are faced with this dilemma of either "a revelation from outside" or "knowledge based on experience". Frequently Christians also experience hesitation and doubt. Of significance here is the new school of "God-is-dead" theologians who hold that because God's existence is not "verifiable"—i.e., in no way whatever falls within reach of controllable experience—all we say about God must be meaningless and nonsensical.[3]

We are undoubtedly faced with a burning question. We might start our search for an answer by looking at the manner in which the older theology treats this problem because the opposition that we observe all around us is provoked precisely by this traditional outlook.

2. *Is Revelation a Supernatural Speaking by God?*

In his *Summa contra Gentiles,* St. Thomas distinguished three ways by which we can know what is divine. The third is the perfect knowledge of God in heaven, which we can leave for the time being in order to limit the discussion to the first two methods. The first of these is a natural way: when "man *ascends* to the knowledge of God by means of created things with the natural light of his reason". The second is supernatural: "insofar as divine truth, which surpasses human reason, *descends* to us by means of revelation".[4] Natural knowledge is here contrasted with revealed knowledge, the ascent of human reason with the descent of divine truth. These contrasts constantly return in later theology.

[2] C. Szczesny, *Die Zukunft des Unglaubens* (Munich, 1958), p. 129.
[3] Cf., among others, P. van Buren, *The Secular Meaning of the Gospel Based on an Analysis of Its Language* (London, 1963).
[4] Thomas Aquinas, *Summa contra Gentiles,* Vol. 4, ch. 1.

To this corresponds the distinction between dogmatic theology, "*what* God has revealed", and apologetics, dealing with the fact "*that* God has revealed". With this it was suggested that "what God has revealed"—i.e., the divine mysteries—remains obscure for our understanding and can only be accepted on authority, in faith, although there undoubtedly occur analogies in dogmatic theology with what we know in a natural manner or analogies that show the interconnection of the mysteries.[5] On the other hand, it was also suggested that the fact of God's revelation could be proved in apologetics by pointing to miracles and prophecies, the life and teaching of Jesus, etc. The fact of revelation, as opposed to its content, could become intelligible to us on the level of our natural reason. Here there was also the distinction between natural knowledge and knowledge by faith, as well as a distinction in the object of these two kinds of knowledge.[6]

This division into two different kinds of knowledge was given its most authoritative confirmation about 100 years ago. Vatican Council I, in its Constitution on the Catholic faith, mentions "a double order of knowledge, different not only in origin but also in object". The origin of one way of knowledge is natural reason; the origin of the other is divine faith. In the light of the first, we know what can be attained by natural reason; in the light of the second, we know the mysteries of faith that can only be apprehended through divine revelation. And so there are two kinds of truths, natural truths and revealed truths. To this the Council added, in conformity with the whole of Catholic theology, a third kind of truths which form, as it were, a bridge between the other two; it stated that, due to divine revelation, those truths of divine revelation that concern the divine, but are not in themselves inaccessible to human reason, can also be known in the present (i.e., fallen) state of man, and this easily, with assurance and without any error.[7]

[5] Vatican Council I; cf. *Denz.* 1796 (3016).
[6] This is of necessity a rather rough outline which would require some modification in detail.
[7] *Denz.* 1795 (3015) and 1786 (3005).

How does God let us know these truths? How does he reveal them, and what truly is revelation? Here theology answers unanimously: revelation is a "supernatural speaking by God". But it is precisely this formulation, together with the division of truths into natural (within the reach of our intelligence) and supernatural (only knowable through revelation), that has provoked so much of the opposition to revelation because it can so easily be misunderstood. In order to understand a little more about the validity (or lack of it) of this opposition, I would like to go back a little further in history.

3. *Earlier Attacks*

The uneasiness about revelation did not arise in our own day or in the recent past. The concept was previously attacked in the 18th century. The Age of Enlightenment meant to deliver man from his tutelage and bring him to intellectual maturity. Whoever wanted to be "enlightened" had to reject every kind of guardianship and only accept as true what he himself could understand. The ideal was to use one's intelligence without being directed by anyone else.[8] Therefore, those unintelligible revealed truths were rejected. Thus there arose various forms of pietism and fideism tending to turn faith into something that had nothing to do with intelligence (e.g., Kant and Schleiermacher), while others attempted to transform the truths of faith into intelligible truths. For these the motto was to move from theology toward philosophy. This was pushed furthest by Hegel who in his

[8] Cf. Kant's well-known definition: "Enlightenment is the process by which man leaves behind the immaturity of which he is himself guilty. Immaturity (*Unmündigkeit*) is the inability to use one's mind without the guidance of someone else. He is himself to blame for this immaturity when the cause does not lie in a lack of intelligence but in a lack of determination and courage that prevents him from using his mind without someone else's guidance. *Sapere aude* (Dare to know). Have the courage to use your own mind—this is the motto of the Enlightenment." Against this statement Kant himself indicated the limits of our intelligence: "I had to give up knowledge [about God] in order to make room for faith."

Philosophy of Religion interpreted all Christian dogmas philo-
sophically. Some Catholic German theologians followed him in
this rather closely. According to Georg Hermes (1775-1831) all
the truths of faith could be understood by man, without any help
of grace, through an "intellectual faith" (*Vernunftglaube*); God's
grace was only necessary for the "faith of the heart" (*Herzens-
glaube*), for the free and total submission of man to God through
which these truths of faith (intellectually understood) became
for him the effective norms of his life. The only starting point
for a responsible faith was doubt, after which one attained certainty through the use of reason.

Vatican Council I, in its Constitution on the Catholic faith,
rightly turned against these theories, but these attacks still continued after 1870. Perhaps, among other things, we should look
for the cause in the overdefensive character of the Constitution.
The Council indeed had coped with a serious danger, but had not
given a constructive answer to a new question. And so the
Modernist crisis at the beginning of our century still centered
around the still unanswered question of the Enlightenment, although formulated slightly differently: Does God's revelation
come "from outside", or have faith and revelation something
(everything?) to do with the self-unfolding of man, with the
way in which he understands himself, with his experience, his
ambitions and dreams of the future? The Modernists became
divided when they developed the theme, but they were united on
the underlying issue. Therefore, they were constantly reproached
for their "immanentism", by which they wanted to understand
everything from within the human being. Unfortunately, the
official ecclesiastical authorities only reacted in a conservative
fashion. They sharply pointed out a number of wrong formulations, but even then offered no constructive answer to the Modernists' very legitimate question. There was no indication for
future development; old positions were maintained and once
more strongly emphasized. In spite of the unsatisfying answers of
the Modernists, their question remains.

4. *Vatican Council II on Revelation*

Against this background it is important to study the *Constitution on Divine Revelation* of Vatican Council II. P. van Leeuwen's article in this issue has already shown that there were sharp differences of opinion on this text, and that the final result differed considerably from the first schema. On some points the first text was even diametrically opposed to the definitive one. Perhaps the most striking difference was the abandonment of the teaching on "the two separate sources of revelation", scripture and tradition, which in the old view were complementary to each other, even in content. Nowhere in the Constitution was it still maintained that tradition contains certain revealed truths that are not in scripture, as was stated explicitly in the preparatory text. However, apart from this difference, which caused an emotional upheaval during the first session, there are others that without doubt are equally important. The whole atmosphere changed. There were no more superfluous and wholly unjustified condemnations of positions held by outstanding Catholic theologians such as Rahner and Benoît. But there was particularly a basic change in the idea of what revelation is. The first schema proposed an idea of revelation that made it almost impossible to meet the objections described at the beginning of this article. There revelation was simply a revelation of truths. It was even explicitly maintained that events such as Christ's death on the cross or his resurrection "do not belong to the order of revelation except by way of the truths hidden in, or linked with, these events insofar as these events are explained by the words of Christ or God's messengers".[9] Revelation was therefore taken to be very exclusively a "supernatural *speaking* by God". The fact that Jesus Christ as a living person is the very Word of God made flesh was apparently meaningless. It was this intel-

[9] "Nam ad revelatum ordinem salutis ii eventus non pertinent, nisi per veritates quae in iis latent aut cum iis connectuntur, sermone Christi et legatorum Dei declarandae atque a nobis fide tenendae": *Schema constitutionis dogmaticae De deposito fidei pure custodiendo*, n. 18.

lectualist approach to revelation as a communication of truths that led to an unqualified condemnation in the first schema of the opinion that "the divine and Catholic faith consists primarily in the experience through which the whole mystery of Christ is perceived, and in him all revealed truth, and secondarily in the act which expresses, by means of concepts and words, what has previously been experienced on a higher level".[10]

This condemnation was not incorporated in the final text. One even has the dizzy feeling of a double somersault when one reads that in the Old Testament God revealed himself, in words and deeds, as the only true and living God to the people he had acquired; thus, Israel was destined to discover by experience which were God's ways with men, to understand them more deeply and clearly day by day when God spoke through the prophets, and to spread their knowledge among the nations.[11] This idea does not greatly differ from what the first schema wanted to condemn. Moreover, diametrically opposed to the preparatory schema, this text clearly states that God does not reveal himself through words only, but through words and deeds. The Constitution insists on this repeatedly so that the deeds are even endowed with a certain priority.[12] Nor are the words considered as revelations by themselves, but it is emphasized that they are inseparably linked with God's deeds and with the fulfillment of his plan for salvation. It is not really surprising, yet most significant, that the Constitution nowhere mentions "revealed truths" in the plural, except in the non-official title of one paragraph which van Leeuwen rightly describes as an unassimilated and almost alien element. If one did not know the

[10] "Proinde teneri non potest fidem divinam et catholicam constitui primarie experientia, qua totum mysterium Christi in eoque omne revelatum verum percipiatur, et secundarie tantum in actu consistere quo, per conceptus et verba, ea exprimantur quae prius altiori gradu experientia attigerit": *ibid.*, n. 20.

[11] *Dogmatic Constitution on Divine Revelation*, n. 14.

[12] Cf. particularly n. 4: "Thus, by all his presence and self-manifestation, by his words and his works, by his symbolic actions and his miracles, especially by his death and his glorious resurrection from the dead, he— the Spirit of truth being finally sent—brings revelation to perfection by fulfilling it, and confirms it with divine witness."

history of all that went before, one might easily overlook the importance of all this, but, particularly in the light of the preparatory schema with its pronounced intellectualism, these facts are very significant. It is also significant that the one paragraph that quotes Vatican Council I so literally stands out as if it did not belong. In shock, one realizes how much the language of the Church in Vatican Council II differs from that of the earlier theology used by Vatican Council I.

Not only did the Constitution overcome the dilemma of "word" or "deed", but it also helped to overcome the dilemma of "God" or "man" and the opposition between "vertical" and "horizontal", between from "without" and from "within". This becomes particularly clear in the treatment of the sacred writings. The human authors of the scriptures are given full recognition. We are encouraged in the text to study the specific style and literary genres of these authors. For the first time these authors, described in previous official documents with great caution as "instrumental authors", are now called and recognized as "true" authors,[13] while at the same time the text fully maintains the fact that God himself is the author of scripture. Biblical research of the last decades has brought out fully the human character of scripture as well as the local, temporal and personal qualification of its presentation and attitudes. However, this does not in any way diminish the fact that God himself wants to speak to us in these human words, and that these truly human words are at the same time God's Word to us.

Even this Constitution undoubtedly leaves a number of *desiderata,* and the question is whether we should expect any Council to have said the last word in theology in any decree, or even to reach the greatest possible theological depth at that particular moment in history. A Council is practically bound to rely too much on compromises, especially if it wants to show some respect for the existing variety of theological opinions within the Church. The great achievement must not be sought primarily in the field of speculative theology but in that of pastoral care,

---

[13] *Ibid.,* n. 11.

as both Pope John XXIII and Pope Paul VI intended. This Council has pulled the Church out of its positions of entrenchment. It has given up the position of unmoving defensiveness. Heeding the Word of God, it has gone out, as Abraham departed from Ur of the Chaldees, in order to face the real problems openly and honestly; the Church now seeks to enter upon a dialogue with the world, even though only the opening sentences speak of an exchange that lies mainly in the future. In the next part of this article I want to develop some thoughts about these first sentences and about those that may possibly follow.

II

SOME FURTHER OBSERVATIONS ON THE PROBLEM

1. *Revelation and Kerygma*

Revelation must not be considered as a communication of independent truths or as something that has nothing to do with the intellect. Dogmas are wholly concerned with faith and revelation. Therefore, it is important to discover the unity of these dogmas and what links them together—i.e., their place in the totality of revelation. One of the best ways to do this it to trace their history and origin and investigate how and when some truths of faith became more prominent—in other words, to study the development of these dogmas.

It has become remarkably clear since 1920, particularly as the result of research in *Formgeschichte,* that a whole explicitation of the faith, comparable to the later development of dogma, had already taken place in the apostolic age. There is no doubt that the oldest apostolic preaching consisted in the proclamation of the resurrection of Jesus. To be an "apostle" was to have been a "witness to his resurrection".[14] When we analyze the historical origin of the gospels, it becomes more and more evident that these gospels essentially do not describe the events and life

[14] Cf., for example, Acts 1, 21-22; 2, 32; 10, 39-43; 1 Cor. 9, 1.

of some dead man whose deeds were remembered with piety, but rather proclaim, like Paul's epistles, the living Lord. They only look to the past, to Jesus' life on earth, in order to proclaim him now as the one who guides toward life, as the Lord who has been raised by God from the dead. One may say without exaggeration that the whole New Testament has been written in the light of faith in Jesus' resurrection, and that all that we can read there is an explicitation of what was already contained in the oldest preaching, the "kerygma", within particular situations.

Insofar as the origins of the gospels are concerned, therefore, the view condemned in the preparatory schema of the Constitution was undoubtedly correct. Faith was not, in the first instance, a set of truths for men to believe in; rather, it sprang from a believing experience and acceptance of the mystery of Christ. The dogmas of the Trinity and the two natures of Christ (which required centuries to clarify), as well as all that is said about incarnation or preexistence in Paul and John, are rooted in, and originate from, this faith in the resurrection and the kerygma.

2. Should Dogmas Be Reinterpreted?

The Easter experience of the apostles is the seed out of which the whole Christian faith developed. This undoubtedly sprang from an inner dynamism, but at the same time it must have been influenced by outward and more accidental circumstances. The apostles and the young Church were bound to express their faith in *their* language, and that does not simply mean Aramaic or Greek but also a way of thinking which, after 2000 years, is no longer exactly the same as ours. The same holds for the later formulations of dogma. We no longer think in the same way as Cyril of Alexandria or the fathers of the Council of Ephesus or of Chalcedon. We even speak a different language from men of the last century, from the bishops that were present at Vatican Council I.

Insofar as the bible is concerned the awareness of this dif-

ference in thought and language has made great progress. Therefore, the Constitution urges us to make a thorough study of the
various literary genres. But one has the impression that this
awareness has made less progress where writings and pronouncements of later ages are concerned. If, guided by critical historical
research and the literary study of the bible, we now read these
texts in a new and fresh manner, should we not expect that
something similar should happen with regard to the formulations
of dogmas that are of a later date?

This is clearly a very delicate business that cannot be handled
with too much respect and prudence. With regard to the Protestant Churches the Church through Pope Paul asked to be for-
given for the part it may have played in the mutual divisions
among Christians. Is it then out of the question that we as
Christians are also partly to blame for the fact that so many of
our contemporaries are no longer Christian? Should we maintain
it to be impossible *a priori* that we can be blamed in some way
for the gap during the last centuries between faith and science—
a gap which now, fortunately, seems diminished? Is there not a
grain of truth in their protest as in that of the Protestants? If
the answer to this question is affirmative, then our guilt does not
merely lie in the fact that we fall short of our religious teaching
in our concrete lives—for example, because of a lack of social
consciousness in our way of thinking and acting. We are also
guilty because we have been clinging too rigidly to our religious
doctrine.

We are confronted with a curious paradox. We reject any re-
interpretation of our dogmas in the name of faith and loyalty to
tradition. But should we not sometimes use a different language
precisely so that we can still say the same thing? For example,
the use of the word "colony" in the centuries before Christ, at
the time of the Greek settlements around the Black Sea, or even
in 1850, quite definitely implied something different from what
we mean by that word today. The successful struggle of the
colonized nations for freedom and independence necessarily
gave this word an unfavorable meaning in later centuries so that

it is now associated with many elements that it did not possess in the past. One can multiply this example by the dozen. Is it then impossible that a man who spoke in the 5th century of the two "natures" of Christ meant something different from what this expression would mean today?

There still remains an entire field to develop for present-day dogmatic theology and the study of the development of dogma. It would be wholly wrong to eliminate all kinds of dogma simply because today we do not know what to do with them. But it would be just as wrong merely to repeat old formulations without modern qualification. Until recently we spoke an unintelligible language in our liturgy. Are we not still speaking a hardly intelligible—and, for our contemporaries, frankly unintelligible—language in matters of faith? The real point is that we must stand in the true tradition and live the same faith in our time as earlier generations did. We cannot *a priori* rule out the fact that this precisely may make it necessary in one way or another to turn away from traditional formulations and structures of thought, even when these have been solemnly proclaimed by councils.

3. *How Do We Overcome the Dilemma: God or Man?*

I have already spoken of a "curious paradox". It is equally noteworthy that the protest of non-Christians against revelation may lead us to a purer notion of what revelation is. Do they not in fact also protest—perhaps even mainly—against a still heathen element in our Christian concept of revelation? The Pythia, prophetess of Apollo, could only transmit the "divine revelation" after having fallen into a trance through poisonous vapors that rose from the cave. Plato even speaks of the visionary's loss of his own spirit before he can become the instrument of the god. In this way he explains the divine "mania" of the prophet (*mantikós*). Here we clearly see the dilemma of God *or* man: man must renounce his own activity to make room for the activity of the deity. Revelation does indeed come about by means of man, but at the same time without what is proper and personal to man. Revelation appears then to be more divine as man himself contributes less to the happening of the revelation. Christianity, however, lives by the mystery of the incarnation: not *either* God *or* man, but *both* God *and* man, in an indissoluble unity of grace.

We now begin to see the truly human aspect of divine revelation and of our faith. We also begin to understand scripture, i.e., the book through which God's Word can reach us, as a genuinely human book. We begin to better realize how a Man from within our history is proclaimed as embodying the fullness of God's revelation. This fully human dimension of revelation reduces the intellectual aspect; it also prevents revelation from being regarded as a communication of truths that God would speak to us, as it were, apart from man, even though by means of man. This raises a number of new problems. But should we not welcome this development as a gain for Christianity?

There is, of course, the danger of going to the other extreme, as is clear from the theories of such Modernists as Tyrrel and Loisy who at the beginning of this century attempted to take the human aspect of revelation too seriously. I do not intend to deal with these theories in detail, but it may be said briefly that they erred in completely severing the experience of faith from the dogmatic formulation of this faith,[15] or in locating Jesus in the growing process of human religious awareness in such a way that there remained little of a divine deed of redemption and, especially, of the unique importance of Jesus for our faith.[16]

[15] Tyrrel maintained this point of view on various occasions. It shows very strongly in his comparison with the thunderbolt. A savage and a scholar see and hear the same thing, he says, but while the savage heard his god thunder, the scholar will express his experience in a completely different way. In the same way there is a complete difference between the experience of revelation and the dogmatic formulation of it in an always fallible theology. One should note that "experience" is here totally related to sense observation. Cf. G. Tyrrel, *Through Scylla and Charybdis, or the Old Theology and the New* (London, 1907), pp. 287-88.

[16] For Loisy revelation was only becoming aware of man's relationship

4. History and Salvation

I have shown in the first part of this article that the Constitution avoids speaking about a "revelation of truths". I developed this thought in the preceding paragraphs and stressed the fact that the Constitution does full justice to the human side (the "real authors"—*veri auctores*) in the growth of the sacred writings traditionally called the "source of revelation". I now will offer some reflections on the unity the Constitution establishes between "God's speaking" and "God's acting". This might help to clarify what has previously been stated.[17]

God's great deed, as proclaimed in the New Testament, is "that God has made him both Lord and Christ, this Jesus whom you crucified",[18] or that "the God of our fathers raised Jesus . . . and exalted him at his right hand as leader and savior, to give repentance to Israel and forgiveness of sins".[19] At the same time it is clear that this gift of the resurrection cannot be detached from Jesus' whole life on earth and especially from his death.

God is not just a supreme idea to which man is led by reflection. He is a living God who has active dealings with us. He is also, and particularly, Lord of history and we must learn to discover his acting in historical events. How?

Often we consider that the ideal knowledge of history lies in as objective an approach as possible to exactly what happened in history—in other words, a reconstruction of history. But when we really begin to see what happened in the past, we also see its significance for the present. Thus, we may look at the life of Socrates, or of John F. Kennedy, or of Pope John, "objectively" and in a "detached" way, and we might call this "historical";

---

with God; Jesus then becomes important because he had such a powerful experience of the fact that man is God's child and God is man's father.

[17] What follows has been greatly influenced by the theology of Rudolf Bultmann, but corrected according to G. Hasenhuettl, *Der Glaubensvollzug. Eine Begegnung mit Rudolf Bultmann aus katholischem Glaubensverständniss* (Essen, 1963), esp. pp. 62-74.

[18] Acts 2, 36.

[19] Acts 5, 30-31.

however, when we really begin to see what these men lived for, we are bound to be affected. Somehow they touch us and their lives turn into an appeal addressed to us. In such a case we are not simply looking at a past phenomenon that at best might be classed as "interesting"; on the contrary, in such a case this particular past puts *us here and now* before a choice, and the past becomes a power in the present that opens up a future. Instead of interested spectators we become people whose existence is inspired by such a past life. From "historians" we become "disciples". The past is then no longer seen as pure "factual history" but as something historically significant—and significant *for us*. When we understand the past in this way, it *reveals* something that is important for us here and now, for our presence in this world, for the way in which we want to realize ourselves.

Scripture never speaks "historically" in the narrow sense. It only mentions the past because, and insofar as, it is significant here and now. Therefore it does not report Jesus' life on earth as if it provided an obituary notice; rather, it speaks of Jesus because he has meaning for those that hear or read.[20]

If we stopped here Jesus—and God's revelation in him—would be nothing more than one of those eminent men human history has known. At most we could say that he means "something more" than the others. But apart from the historical element (that this man really lived in this way at that time) and the *geschichtliche* element (the significance of this life for us here and now), there is a third element that belongs properly to Jesus' life, death and resurrection—namely, the eschatological or final and definitive element: the divine dimension. The life of Jesus that is proclaimed to us does not offer us merely one

---

[20] This is also the deepest reason why the gospels do not report everything as it happened "factually"—i.e., in outward appearance. One may compare this with a work of art: no artist reproduces purely the outward appearance of what is seen or heard. Everything has passed through his spirit, his artist's vision, and that is precisely what makes his work a work of art. We can only appreciate it if we enter into his spirit. Thus, in scripture all events are seen in the spirit of faith, which puts into relief its deepest significance; therefore, we can also understand the scriptures only if we enter into this spirit of faith.

choice among others. We believe that he is not merely a word; he is proclaimed as THE Word, with a decisive, final and definitive meaning for us. Therefore the proclamation of Jesus has three dimensions for us, presenting a total choice that involves our whole human existence. Whoever accepts this proclamation of Jesus' life, death and resurrection, and becomes his "disciple" in the full sense of the word, is no longer the person he formerly was. He becomes a *kaine ktisis*,[21] a "new creation" and passes from sin to righteousness;[22] he is no longer "of this world" [23] because he has put down the old Adam[24] and is born again in Christ.[25] All these expressions show the eschatological character of God's revelation in Jesus Christ, and thus indicate the unique place of Jesus for our faith.

Must we simply accept this, or can we also experience it? It is clear that the early Christians really understood that this preaching presented them with a total choice, for it was from this experience that they wrote down those testimonies mentioned in the previous paragraph. And wherever there is genuine Christian witnesses, this experience, rooted in the mystery of the person of Jesus Christ, will be present.

5. *Initial Perception and Understanding of Revelation*

Christian revelation is unique in the history of religion in that it does not give us profound and timeless truths about man, but is rather a revelation in and through history—hence the unique connection in it of "words and deeds". But does it not also tell us something "new", something that surpasses our intelligence?

Something new is indeed communicated in revelation. But what we come to see as new in faith is less concerned with mysteries beyond our understanding than with the fact that revelation *does* take place, that for centuries and even from the beginning of

---

[21] Cf. 2 Cor. 5, 17; Gal. 6, 15.
[22] Cf. Rom. 3, 21-30.
[23] Cf. Jn. 17, 14-16.
[24] Eph. 4, 22; cf. Eph. 4, 24; Rom. 6, 2-13.
[25] Cf. Jn. 3, 3-8.

creation what all generations of men and particularly the old
Israel awaited is actually happening. It is precisely the *fact* of
revelation that the glad tidings of the Gospel proclaim. Therefore, it is dangerous to distinguish between "*what* God reveals"
and "*that* God reveals"; the first would be beyond rational
demonstration but not the second. It would be better to reverse
the proposition: all generations of mankind and especially the
people of Israel have longed for revelation and redemption.
Every man clearly has somewhere an idea of what revelation
and redemption are, in the form of some (possibly inarticulate)
hunch or antecedent perception. How else could he long for
redemption? However, what is proclaimed to us is the *fact that*
God redeems us. The Gospel is not a "glad doctrine" but "glad
tidings", the proclamation of a long-expected fact of salvation—
however necessary it may be afterward for this fact of salvation
to be expressed in a doctrine.

The redemption undoubtedly also redeems and purifies our
antecedent perception of revelation. It then becomes a true understanding, and faith is then described as a new "light" that
shines for us. One might compare this with friendship. Everyone
has some idea about friendship, but when one meets a real friend
this understanding of friendship becomes wholly new, much
deeper and existential. His guesses and previous notions then
pass into understanding. In all probability he will then also have
to revise and correct all his earlier, more theoretical notions
about friendship; nevertheless, what is then fulfilled is precisely
what he had hoped for earlier, perhaps subconsciously.

In a similar way revelation must be proclaimed in such a way
that people can understand it and recognize it as what they
longed for deep in their heart and with their whole person. Only
when there is this recognition, and when revelation is no longer
seen as something that comes completely "from outside" but
rather as the merciful fulfillment of man's profoundest hope—
only then can the proclamation of God's redemptive deed have
the force to make really "new men" of us. Only then it will be
"God's Word" to us in the full sense of the expression, in power
creating us anew.

Anton Vögtle/*Freiburg im Br., W. Germany*

Revelation and History in the New Testament: Biblical Hermeneutics

During the last few decades, the hermeneutic question has advanced markedly into the foreground of discussion.[1] Today there is general recognition of certain conditions and requirements for scriptural exegesis, particularly of the New Testament. Among these recognized preconditions is the necessity of full comprehension by the interpreter of the bible. The exposition of historical texts—biblical texts in particular—is indeed not only a question of the correct handling of the relevant scientific historical aids and methods. Experience shows that the possession of the same sources and a unanimous recognition of the same scientific historical procedures have not as yet led to a unanimously agreed exposition of the bible. These by themselves cannot guarantee an "objective" exegesis or an adequate understanding of the Good News contained in the New Testament. The enlightened concept of an absolutely unprejudiced approach to historical texts has been shown to be purely imaginary. Those who read and expound the bible documents today come to it from their own concrete historical situation, and bring to the task a body of innate preconceptions that have grown out of their own personal development and situation in

[1] H. Schnackenburg gives a list of recent Catholic and Protestant contributions in his essay "Zur Auslegung der Heiligen Schrift in unserer Zeit," in *Bibel und Leben* 5 (1964), pp. 220-36; cf. especially footnote 1.

life, or their own particular "school". On this basis they interrogate their source material and seek to come to a general understanding of the phenomena to which the New Testament bears witness. This has been most impressively demonstrated to the exegetes of all Confessions by R. Bultmann's scheme of interpretation, in which he develops a unified hermeneutical principle based upon definite axiomatic assumptions.

1. *An Indispensable Prior Decision*

The New Testament proclaims the decisive abrogation of the Old Testament in which a personal God revealed himself by the coming of Jesus Christ and claims that this message is the final word for the understanding and fulfillment of human existence.[2] It therefore belongs to the nature of this message, as proclaimed in the bible and the New Testament in particular, that this prior understanding should be of supreme importance. And so, no exegete can avoid a prior decision—whether unwitting or fully conscious—on this question of principle raised by our theme of "revelation and history". We refer to the question whether, and in what sense, God could reveal himself, whether God's action could be objectified in an historically demonstrable event—i.e., in the life and destiny of an historical person—and whether he could communicate this event as such to mankind. The exegesis of the New Testament necessarily leads to different interpretative attitudes. On the one hand, the expositor may exclude the possibility of an objective self-revelation by God in history because of some restriction of his prior understanding of the matter through the limitations of what would appear to be possible to contemporary thought; on the other hand, his philosophical convictions or his faith may lead him to reckon with a living God and Lord of nature and history with whom such action is possible, and so compel him to recognize this action in the sense and to the extent

[2] Cf. especially H. Schlier, "Was heisst Auslegung der Heiligen Schrift?" in *Besinnung auf das Neue Testament, Exegetische Aufsätze und Vorträge II* (Freiburg im Br., 1964), pp. 35-62.

that the documents to be expounded demand. Only one who remains open to the possibility that God could impart himself in
history in the shape of an historical Person will, for example,
be able to construe Jesus' message to mean that Jesus not only
proclaimed in a purely "prophetical" way—in an existential
sense—the coming of the kingdom of God and the Son of Man,[3]
but that he did truly interpret his own words and actions as the
real beginning of the promised final redemptive action of God,
and that the Jesus of human history therefore claimed to be
the final revealer and mediator of the redemption that belonged
to the last days.[4] Only one who recognizes this claim as fulfilling
an historical mission will be able to consider it reasonable and
credible that Jesus performed "mighty acts"—immediately raising the question of how many and what particular "miracles" in
the gospels are to be actually accepted—and that Jesus himself
regarded these as the most outstanding and compelling manifestation of the eschatological action of God which was now
entering its final stages.

2. An Inadequate Conception of the History of Revelation in Christ

This preliminary question of principle by no means exhausts
the hermeneutical relevance of the theme of "revelation and history". In order to explore this, let us start from a very unre-
flecting conception of the history of Christ's revelation which still
exercises a powerful effect. According to this view, God most
certainly revealed his will to bring holiness and salvation in the

[3] Among others, R. Bultmann, G. Bornkamm, W. Marxsen and E.
Tödt; cf. R. Formesyn, "Was There Pronominal Connection for the 'Bar
Nasha' Self-designation?" in Novum Testamentum 8 (1966), pp. 1-35.
On the other hand it is doubted by others (E. Käsemann, P. Vielhauer,
H. Conzelmann) whether Jesus ever used the title "Son of Man"; cf.
H. Teeple, "The Origin of the Son of Man Christology," in Journal of
Biblical Literature, 84 (1965), pp. 213-250.
[4] For a comprehensive view, cf. R. Schnackenburg, Gottes Herrschaft
und Reich, with a supplement (Freiburg im Br., ⁴1965), pp. 79-109;
O. Cullmann, Heil als Geschichte (Tubingen, 1965), pp. 167-214.

framework of the history of a particular people, and finally in the history of Jesus of Nazareth. But this story of Christ's revelation is foreshortened to imply that Jesus and even God himself (cf. Mk. 1, 10f.) in all his earthly activities, and to some extent from the first moment of his appearance, proclaimed—and was bound to proclaim exactly in substance and in manner—what the apostles proclaimed after Easter and Pentecost, and what is to be read in the New Testament. According to this view, the apostles were only repeating what Jesus had proclaimed and taught up to Good Friday, or, indeed, up to the end, when he spoke as the risen Lord. This simplified idea of the whole conception, which is incidentally not at all difficult to grasp,[5] certainly expresses a genuine and indeed very essential point of view. Nevertheless, it is inadequate because it fails to do justice to the historical character of revelation at a crucial point. The continuity between the Good News that followed Easter and the message of Jesus that led up to it cannot be represented simply as a material identity, in the sense of a mechanical and external repetition.

3. *The Hermeneutical Relevance of the Genuinely Historical Character of Revelation in Christ*

The question of the relationship between the historical Jesus and the Christ of faith has understandably enough been discredited, having been posed in the sharpest terms by the demythologizing existential theologians, and answered by counter claims that an objective revelation really took place in historical events. But while rejecting this line of interpretation, one must not overlook the fact that the distinction between the Jesus who proclaimed and the Jesus who was proclaimed is in a true sense justifiable, and in fact required, by the very events of revelation in Christ. Not only the revelation of the Old Testament was ful-

---

[5] A. Vögtle, *Das Neue Testament und die neuere katholische Exegese I* (Freiburg im Br., 1966), pp. 68-73.

filled as genuine history which both looked forward and led forward. In accordance with God's plan of salvation, the fulfillment of revelation in and through Jesus was a genuinely historical and progressive process that made use of secondary causes. It displays itself as a process including not only the history of Jesus in the strict sense of the word—that is, the life and activity of Jesus that ended on Good Friday—but also, and of equal importance, the resulting events concerning Jesus from which his coming to life again draws its revelatory significance. For the exegesis of the New Testament and for a reasoned basis and understanding of revelation in Jesus Christ, it is of great importance to take account of the genuinely progressive historical character belonging to these events. By way of illustration, we can only call attention here to one or two detailed points.

4. The Revelatory Character of Jesus' Earthly Life

According to the three older gospels, which bear firm witness to the characteristic theme and form of the message, Jesus only laid down one condition for Israel's entry into the kingdom of God: namely, the faithful and penitent reception of his message, which required the fulfillment of the religious and moral demands that he conclusively and bindingly revealed. Indeed, the whole tenor of his message implies that the coming of the kingdom of God and the Son of Man is a genuine possibility that precisely demands this immediate and lasting conversion and a state of watchful "readiness". But Jesus did not, in effect, say to the Israelites: "If you would enter the kingdom, it is not enough that you should open your hearts to the message of God's will to save and sanctify you which I have come to proclaim." Rather did he say: "I must die for you or for 'many', and not until then will you be able to draw upon the cleansing power of my death [in the sacrament of baptism]." This prophecy in advance is not what we should expect either, for it would have been just as much a weakening of the demands that he had publicly made in Israel for conversion and watchful readiness as would have been an express or implied promise of a mission to the Gentiles that must precede the coming of the end.[6]

If this observation is correct, it would be premature—nay, positively untenable—to conclude that Jesus never could have intended to take a new step in the announcement of salvation or set up a new constitution for the saved community. True, he neither grouped all the Israelites who were ripe for conversion together nor set them apart in an organization separate from the rest of Israel, but he could not consistently have done this as long as he was intending to prepare all Israel to be the heirs of salvation, regardless of any greater or lesser degree in which they were righteous or fulfilled the Law. Nor did he speak in public about his intention to found a new Church. Yet it would be arbitrary to seek to confine the redemptive and saving work of Jesus simply to his proclamation of the religious and moral requirements of his kingdom, and exclude the possibility that Jesus himself recognized in the fateful death that was bearing down upon him a divine "necessity" that was going to add something to his present power to save.

In order to grasp the saving power of Jesus' life on earth in all its completeness and with all its apparent contradictions, the expositor of the New Testament, in spite of the textual criticism demanded by the peculiar character of his sources, will have to give full weight to the genuinely historical—that is, the progressive—character of the revelation in Christ and treat this as an essential point of view.

In concrete terms, therefore, he will have to seriously consider the possibility, on the one hand, that God in the earthly life of Jesus was respecting the redemptive privileges of Israel as the first and immediate heirs of the promise; equally, on the other hand, he must weigh the possibility that God had reckoned on the rejection of the revealer by the rulers of the people and worked it into his plan of salvation—nay, that he even made use

[6] A. Vögtle, "Exegetische Erwägungen über das Wissen und Selbstbewusztsein Jesu," in *Gott in Welt, Festgabe fur K. Rahner*, I, pp. 620-26.

of this very decision to set in motion a new act of redemption that should make possible a new initiative in proclaiming the Good News and a new constitution for the saved community (Mt. 16, 18). In this sense we should also interpret the actual, but by no means obvious, development of the mission to the Gentiles subsequent to Easter as an altogether divinely intended further step in the revelation of Christ. We can hardly explain the critical voice and the missionary role of the "Hellenists" as mere chance, nor can we interpret the later commission of Paul by the risen Lord as a mere later insertion to help out the story, necessitated by the failure or the unexpected reluctance of the first apostle. Such an explanation would hardly fit in with the conception of a divine economy in the plan of revelation and salvation.

5. *The Revelatory Act of the Resurrection*

Quite apart from the debatable questions concerning the extent to which Jesus in his earthly life foretold the victorious outcome of his encounter with death, or how far he himself prophesied his parousia as the Son of Man returning in judgment and foresaw for himself an existence and activity after death at the right hand of God, the story of Jesus certainly did not come to an end with his ignominious execution on the gallows. According to the firm conviction of the apostles, it began afresh through a new and mighty act of revelation on the part of God which raised it to a different plane from that of the earthly life, and which continued through the glorified life of the Lord in his Church. According to the unanimous witness of the New Testament, the disciples became firmly convinced through the revelation vouchsafed to them by Jesus in his post-resurrection appearances that God had answered the execution of Jesus by raising him again to life, which they saw as a purely miraculous event, and that this both confirmed his claims to have a message for the last days and exalted him above death into a position of divine power at the right hand of God in his heavenly kingdom. This revelatory act of God was both the basis of the decisive role of

Jesus in bringing in the final age of salvation (Marana-tha), and the apostolate that was to lead up to the establishing of a divine head of the Church and the sending of the Holy Spirit. The fact that critical considerations make it impossible to establish an original wording for the logia spoken by the risen master to the same extent that is possible for the words of the earthly Jesus only confirms the miraculous character of his post-resurrection appearances. It does not justify the slightest doubts about the preeminent revelatory significance ascribed with one unanimous voice by the New Testament to the encounters with the risen Lord. Moreover, the *Dogmatic Constitution on Divine Revelation* expressly points to the revelatory importance of the raising from the dead: ". . . the apostles reported to their audiences the things which he had said and done, with the fuller insight which they enjoyed, one they had learned from Christ's glorious destiny, and they were enlightened by the Spirit of truth" (n. 19).

The climax and turning point of the revelation in Christ constituted by the resurrection has a hermeneutical relevance that must not be overlooked. Although our New Testament documents do not in any way set out to write a history of the revelation in Christ, all in their different ways focus attention upon the resurrection (e.g., Mk. 9, 9f.; Jn. 2, 22; 7, 39; 12, 16; 16, 12f.). The interpretation of these writings must start out afresh from the experience of the risen master if the way that leads to his exaltation (Lk. 24, 25-27) and the worth of the Messiah (Acts 1, 3) is to be set upon a proper footing and made intelligible. And so, from the christological and salvational status achieved through death and resurrection there stretches forth a progressive interpretation and unfolding of the story of Jesus largely based upon scripture, as the New Testament documents plainly demonstrate.

(a) *The Successive Unfolding of the Revelation in Christ*

Once again we can only indicate a few points by way of illustration. Take for example the interpretation of Jesus' resurrection based upon Old Testament passages (2 Sam. 7, 14; Pss. 2, 7; 110, 1; Is. 45, 33), regarding it as promotion to the messianic sonship,[7] as placement at the right hand of God,[8] and as enthronement as almighty "Lord", to be worshiped as divine.[9] If this initial christology of exaltation is directed to establishing the firm basis in scripture of Jesus' position of messianic power that will make possible his coming in a final revelation (which is clearly demanded by the underlying theme of the doctrine), the pre-Pauline kerygmatic *paradosis* in 1 Corinthians 15, 3f. also includes the specifically redemptive meaning of Jesus' death—his dying "for our sins"—as part of that which took place "according as it was written". This interest of finding in scripture the reasoned basis and the unfolding of the saving power of the passion also explains the efforts made in this direction by even the oldest account of the passion. In order to prevent any idea of a culpable disaster, the events of the passion are presented mostly in indirect or allusive scriptural phraseology as "the fulfillment and unveiling of all the sufferings of the Servant of God and of all the Old Testament saints", and thus as the divinely-planned way to exaltation.[10] In the same way the explicit and kerygmatic formulation of the theme of suffering and resurrection in prophecy is really the center and major emphasis of the oldest gospel writings (cf. Mk. 8, 27ff.).

To take another example, it is only on the ground of the great reversal of the resurrection that the Davidic origin of Jesus and his entrance into the messianic sonship (his enthronement as Lord and ruler) are interpreted as the basis of two different modes of existence—namely, the earthly and human, and the heavenly and spiritual, lives of Jesus. And so, from the exaltation of Jesus as divine Lord, which stands in the strongest contrast to the earthly life ending in death, the apostolic proclamation pauses and looks back beyond the birth of the Messiah as it seeks reflec-

[7] Rom. 1, 4; Acts 13, 33; cf. Heb. 1, 5f.; 5, 5.

[8] Rom. 8, 34; Col. 3, 1; Eph. 1, 20; Acts 2, 33-35; 5, 31; 7, 56; 1 Pet. 3, 21f.; Heb. 1, 13; 13, 1; cf. Mk. 14, 62.

[9] Phil. 2, 9-11; cf. Mt. 28, 18.

[10] H. Schlier, *op. cit.*, p. 55.

tively to plumb the depths of the events focused in Christ. Linking up at the same time, it seems, with the Jewish-Hellenistic doctrine of the creative wisdom, it unfolds the unique sonship claimed by Jesus, qualifying him to be the absolute revealer (Mt. 11, 27) and so leads on to the recognition of his preexistence (Phil. 2, 6ff.; 1 Cor. 8, 6; 10, 4; Col. 1, 15ff.; Jn. 1, 1ff.), and thence to the incarnation of the preexistent Son of God (Gal. 4, 4f.; Rom. 1, 3; 8, 3; Jn., *passim*). Not until after Easter are the consequences of the mystery of the crucified drawn out, the exaltation of Christ to be the Lord who gives his life for the world, as they affect the existence and the life of the individual man in the Church and in the whole cosmos. At this point the revelatory presuppositions have been sufficiently set out for the unfolding of a theology of salvation, a baptismal theology of the type witnessed to by Romans 6, a Pauline Christ-mysticism, a mysticism of God and Christ as set forth in St. John. Not until this point can the teaching of the Church as the body of Christ be developed, the ecclesiological and cosmological significance of Christ in the sense of Colossians and Ephesians, or even of Hebrews. Thus it is only the recognition of a divinely ordered progress in the divine action leading to the revelation in Jesus Christ that makes it possible to present a satisfactory explanation of the peculiar relationship between the Gospel's (particularly the synoptic) Good News and that contained in the extra-evangelical writings, and especially to make sense of the fact that the post-Easter message is also stronger than that of the earthly Jesus' "evangelium über Jesus Justus". From the hermeneutical point of view, it is clearly unjustifiable to postulate a more or less material identity between the Jesus who proclaims and the Jesus who is proclaimed, and so to demand that all the incidents in the post-Easter message, if they are to be regarded as genuine revelation, be shown to be explicit, or at least implicit, in the words and deeds of the earthly Jesus.

(b) *The Peculiar Revelational Character of the Gospel Account of Jesus*

On the other hand, the genuinely historical and progressive character of the revelation in Christ results in the unique form of the oral and written accounts of Jesus in that they do not simply tell the story of Jesus retrospectively, as though reproducing a record of events and an easily intelligible train of cause and effect. First, a word as to the manner in which the gospels apply the moral to the story and give it contemporary meaning. Because Jesus was for the apostolic generation not only a "past" figure, but also and primarily a present, highly alive and active personality—one who could be prayed to and was present with them in worship, one who continued to work in the power of the Spirit, teaching, promising, warning, binding them under obligations, pouring forth his life upon them—the primitive Church also interpreted all that it had to proclaim in the way of instruction upon the details of the story of Jesus as a Word that made him present, a Word addressed here and now to the faithful by the exalted Lord in the situation that was rooted in Good Friday, Easter and Pentecost. In the second place, it is easy to see how the recognition of the events of Christ's life, culminating in his exaltation, also began to develop, sometimes more and sometimes less, into an interpretative reproduction of the words, deeds and data from the life story of Jesus, so that St. John's gospel, to the extent that it was a witness of these events, could include the remaining revelatory events—the death, the resurrection and the sending of the Holy Spirit—in the Word of the earthly Jesus. As long as we grant full validity to the progressive character of the revelation in Christ and see this as a hermeneutical principle, this strong kerygmatizing of the earthly life of Jesus not only loses any objectionable character, but is seen to be a decisive protest against all attempts to deprive the Gospel of its historical basis or to dissipate the revelation in Jesus Christ into some Gnostic mirage.

St. John's gospel emphatically includes and interprets the

status of Lord and savior achieved by Christ after the resurrection as part and parcel of the Word of the earthly Jesus, so that the present moment of the earthly life and the future activities of the exalted Christ interpenetrate one another to an extent that far exceeds anything to be found in the Synoptists. This must be seen as a particularly impressive proof of the early Church's conviction that the events beginning with the incarnation or the public ministry of Jesus and culminating in the exaltation and the sending of the Spirit were all part of a unified divine plan of salvation, laid down and worked out systematically in the divine dispensation, and moving forward to a final fulfillment that was still to come.

6. *The Hermeneutic Relevance of the Action of the Holy Spirit*

The message of the New Testament extends to the end of the 1st century and was delivered under the most varied conditions—christological, soteriological, sacramental, ecclesiological, moral and religious—and it witnesses to a successive unfolding of the events concerning Christ. In view of these facts, a final and essential hermeneutical question arises: Who can guarantee the correctness and truthfulness of this unfolding of the revelation in Christ? This question is answered by the New Testament in a variety of settings by pointing to this same truth, with all its revelatory and salvational importance—the action of the Holy Spirit, through whom the exalted Christ is present and powerfully at work.[11] Admittedly, at this point the appeal to the Spirit as the preserver and continuer of the revelation in Christ marks the boundary line of what can be stated as fact and solidly based upon reason, a line that must inevitably be reached by any scientifically historical exposition of the New Testament. In the nature of the case, as far as the revelation in Christ is concerned, the exegete working by scientific historical methods

[11] 1 Cor. 2, 10f.; 7, 40; 2 Cor. 3, 17f.; Lk. 24, 48; Acts 1, 4; 2, 33; Jn. 7, 39; 14, 15ff. 26f.; 16, 7. 13ff.; 20, 21f.; Mt. 28, 20.

should be required, with due deference to historical-critical requirements, to demonstrate in positive fashion that the Holy
Spirit was in command of the unfolding of the revelation in
Christ clearly perceptible in the New Testament, and so guarantee its absolute concreteness and truth. But it must be considered
quite pertinent for the exegete to point to the New Testament
claim that the Holy Spirit exercises a preservative and expository
function and adopt this as a hermeneutical principle. He may
certainly consider himself justified in critically protesting the
contention that a process was already at work distorting the New
Testament documents and introducing into them heterogene-
ous elements. Moreover, he can go further than this, for he will
be able to recognize the development of revelation in Christ witnessed to by the New Testament as inwardly coherent and legitimate, insofar as he is able to bring to his task a faithful conviction of the preservative and expository action of the exalted Lord
through the influence of the Holy Spirit.

Juan Alfaro, S.J. / *Rome, Italy*

The Dual Aspect of Faith: Entrusting Oneself to God and Acceptance of the Christian Message

I

THE BIBLICAL CONCEPT OF FAITH

St. Paul sees faith as the action of man receiving the grace of justification from God through Christ.[1] According to St. John, the believer possesses "eternal life"; he participates through Christ in the very life of God.[2] The Council of Trent, in full accord with both Pauline and Johannine theology, defined faith as the fundamental dimension of the Christian life.[3] This unchanging emphasis on the primordial importance of faith means that we must first of all ask ourselves the question: What, *essentially*, is faith?

Vatican Council II has formulated a definition of faith that sounds surprising in its novelty of terms, though in fact it is only an explanation of the teaching of Vatican Council I: "To God who reveals himself is due the 'obedience of faith' by which man freely pledges himself to God, giving 'God the full submission of his intelligence and will', and voluntarily assenting to the revelation he has made." "Man's response to God in faith must be free. . . . The act of faith is by its very nature a free act. Man . . . called to be God's adopted son, cannot give his

[1] Rom. 3, 22-31; 4, 1-22; 5, 1; 9, 30. 32; Gal. 2, 16; 3, 10-26.
[2] Jn. 3, 16. 36; 5, 24-26; 6, 40. 47; 10, 28; 11, 25; 14, 6; 15, 5; 17, 3; 20, 31.
[3] Sess. III, cap. 8 (Denz-Schönm. 1532).

53

adherence to God revealing himself, unless the Father draws him
to offer to God the reasonable and free submission of faith." [4]

According to the Council, the act of faith proceeds from
man's whole spiritual dynamic, from his understanding and his
will; it includes assent to the content of revelation, obedience to
the divine Word and confidence in God who saves us through
Christ. By faith man entrusts himself to God's grace and enters
into communion of life with him.

Vatican Council II's definition is fully in accord with the
biblical concept of faith. In the Old Testament the act of faith is
described as "putting one's faith" or "trust" in the Lord,[5] as man
entrusting himself to the saving Word of God. "Putting his faith"
in God, Abraham entrusted himself to the divine promise (Gen.
15, 1-6; 16, 1; cf. Rom. 4, 20). Israel arose as a people with
faith in Yahweh, the God of the covenant—that is, it knew his
saving power, accepted his sovereignty and entrusted itself to
his protection (Exod. 4, 1-31; 14, 10-18; Num. 1, 4-41). The
doctrine of the one God was a result of Israel's religious experience, of Yahweh having revealed himself in Israel's history as the
only savior: *Yahweh alone is God, because he alone can save.*
The *understanding* character of faith was then consciously emphasized (Is. 43, 10-12). The knowledge of God, preached
by the prophets, included the profession of faith in one God
(Hos. 2, 20; Is. 45, 5. 22; Jer. 24, 7; Exod. 6, 7-13) which
was fixed in set formulas (Deut. 6, 20-24; 26, 5-9; Jos. 24, 2-
13).

The Church was born with faith in the saving facts of the
death and resurrection of Jesus (Acts 2, 14-36; 3, 12-26; 4,
9-12; 5, 29-32; 10, 34-43). The oldest formulas of Christian
faith proclaimed Christ as the "Lord" (Phil. 2, 11; 1 Cor. 12,
3; Rom. 10, 9). In St. Paul faith and the message correspond to

---

[4] *Dogmatic Constitution on Divine Revelation*, n. 5; *Declaration on
Religious Freedom*, n. 10. Cf. Vatican Council I, Sess. III, cap. 3 (Denz-
Schönm. 3008, 3010, 3035).

[5] Gen. 15, 6; Exod. 14, 31; Num. 14, 11; 20, 12; 2 Kg. 17, 14;
Is. 43, 10; Jon. 3, 5; Deut. 1, 32; 9, 23; Pss. 78, 22; 106, 12. 24; 2 Chr.
20, 20.

each other as the affirmation and its content (1 Cor. 15, 1-18; 3, 5; Rom. 13, 11; 2 Thess. 4, 18); the term *pístis,* which originally meant the act of believing, came to mean the message believed (Rom. 10, 8; Gal. 1, 23; Eph. 4, 5; Acts 6, 7; 13, 8). Faith is primarily the acceptance of the Christian message, but it also includes man's submission to the grace of Christ (Rom. 10, 17; 2, 8; 2 Cor. 9, 13; 2 Thess. 1, 8-10) and confidence in God's love, shown in the sacrifice of his Son (Rom. 4, 18-20; 5, 9; 6, 8; 8, 31-36; Eph. 3, 12; 2 Cor. 2, 14-18). In St. John, faith is knowing Christ as the Son of God, sent by the Father to give eternal life to men (Jn. 8, 24-28; 10, 38; 14, 12-20; 17, 3. 8. 21. 23), but this is knowledge that involves man's total adherence to the person of Christ and sharing in his life (Jn. 10, 14-27; 17, 8. 21-25; 1 Jn. 2, 23-24; 4, 7-15).

Modern exegesis recognizes that, in both the Old and the New Testaments, faith is man's total response to God who reveals himself as the savior, and this response includes both acceptance of God's message of salvation and confident submission to his Word. In the faith of the Old Testament the emphasis is more on confidence, while in the New Testament it is more on assent to the Christian message.[6]

II

FAITH: ACCEPTANCE OF THE CHRISTIAN MESSAGE

Christian faith is wholly dependent on the saving intervention of God through the death and resurrection of his Son: "If Christ has not risen, all your faith is a delusion; you are back in your sins" (1 Cor. 15, 14-17). If the resurrection is a fact, then Christianity exists; if it is not, then Christianity does not. If faith

[6] Cf. E. Jacob, *Théologie de l'Anc. Test.* (Neuchâtel, 1955), pp. 141-45; P. van Imschoot, "Fe," in *Diccionario de la Biblia* (Barcelona, 1963), pp. 686-91; R. Schnackenburg, "Glaube," in *Lex. Theol. u. Kirche* IV, pp. 913-17; J. Alfaro, "Fides in terminologia biblica," in *Gregorianum* 42 (1961), pp. 463-505; A. Weiser and R. Bultmann, "πιστευω," in *Theol. Wörterb. z. N.T.* VI, pp. 174-230.

fails to grasp the fact of the resurrection, then it fails to grasp the reality of salvation. But the resurrection cannot be grasped as a fact except in the form of a message, the affirmation of a proposition. If faith rises to the reality of the saving mystery of Christ, it is bound to include intellectual assent to the message which proclaims the reality of this mystery. The Christian message, as a human message expressed in images and concepts, inevitably has a doctrinal context, but this context is itself the vehicle of the very reality of salvation through Christ. Christianity is not primarily, or ultimately, a doctrine; it is the person of the Son of God, made man, who died and rose again for the salvation of all mankind.

Man can only be saved through participation in the saving mystery of Christ (Acts 4, 2; Rom. 1, 16; 3, 22-28; 6, 1-9; 10, 9-10; Jn. 3, 14; 16, 36), but he cannot participate in this mystery without an inner conviction of its reality, without believing it to be true. The intellectual nature of faith corresponds to the real nature of the mystery of Christ; without this intellectual aspect the mystery ceases to be real. Faith lives on the reality of its object, which is God's saving intervention through Christ. If the saving event of Christ is not real *in itself*, it cannot be real *for me* either, and so cannot be lived as real (Gal. 2, 20; Rom. 4, 24-25; 2 Cor. 5, 15).

Ultimately, the whole doctrinal content of Christianity expresses the saving intervention of God through Christ. The mystery of the Trinity and the mystery of the Church have been revealed in the mystery of Christ. The whole of revelation converges on Christ and has its definitive truth in him. Thus every act of faith (whatever its particular content) has the mystery of our salvation through Christ as its ultimate object.

The doctrinal aspect of faith is inseparable from its ecclesial aspect. Unity in faith is vital to the Church (Eph. 4, 5), for without communion in one believed reality it would not be the community of believers. This communion is not possible without the transmission of revelation through society, and this must be expressed in definite forms if it is to be preached. The ecclesial message which binds the Church together needs to be accepted as true by the faith of Christians. The Church could not be the visible community of those who believe in Christ if the act of faith did not include acceptance of a definite doctrinal content.

III

FAITH: ENTRUSTING ONESELF TO GOD

In the Christian message God comes to meet man, holding out the free gift of his love and demanding absolute trust from man in return. In the final analysis, faith is not just acceptance of a doctrine, but rather of the reality expressed in the doctrine, the gift of himself by God as our Father in Christ. Man's freedom to accept the grace of salvation corresponds to the sovereign freedom of the saving initiative of God. By revealing himself in his Son, God has called man to live in intimate proximity to him; man responds to this call through faith and puts himself under the power of God's grace.

Entrusting oneself to God in obedience and confidence is not a marginal aspect of faith but its very nucleus. By giving us absolute proof of his love in the sacrifice of his own Son, God calls us to absolute trust in his mercy (Rom. 5, 8-10; 8, 31-39). Faith in God who saves us through Christ can hardly fail to include trust in him. The mystery of the love of God, who gave us his own Son and who calls us to participate through him in his own divine life (Jn. 3, 16; 1 Jn. 3, 1-2; 4, 9-15), is something that transcends our intelligence; if we are to accept it in faith we have to make the daring and trusting surrender of our existence to God who is absolute love and absolute mystery. "In this hope we are saved" (Rom. 8, 24); our salvation has already been realized by Christ, but our own commitment to participation in the glory of the Lord has not yet been realized. Faith orients our lives toward our meeting with Christ in glory beyond death (Rom. 8, 23; 2 Cor. 5, 8; Phil. 1, 23; 3, 10-12; 1 Thess,

4, 17; Heb. 11, 1; 9, 28; Jn. 17, 24; 1 Jn. 3, 2); underlying this orientation is our trusting hope in the grace of Christ.

When he believes in God (the first aspect of faith) man bases his belief on God's divine veracity (Jn. 3, 33)—that is, he trusts him as a witness absolutely worthy of trust. At the same time he submits himself to the authority of his divine Word. When God speaks, he speaks as God and his Word must be accepted by man.

The demands of Christianity—its absolute character, the imitation of Christ based on the Law of God and the cross, the life of the Christian oriented toward its final fulfillment—also force man to an unequivocal exercise of his freedom. Faith in Christ is a radical and irrevocable decision (Lk. 11, 23; 8, 22; Mk. 9, 43-47; Mt. 5, 1-48). It is not so much an act or series of acts as a basic, all-embracing attitude of mind which imposes a definite direction on the whole of one's life. Man, called by grace to intimacy with God, produces the decision from the depths of his freedom, and it embraces his whole personality— intelligence, will and action (submission to the mystery, love and law of Christ).

It is officially stated by the magisterium of the Church that if man breaks his friendship with God through sin, his faith does not necessarily disappear. But this does not mean that faith can exist without desire for the love of God. Faith necessarily implies desire for salvation, born of the reconciliation of man to God in the beatific vision. Faith reaches its fullness as faith when it is love of God, made present in love of man. If charity is lacking, faith itself is mortally wounded, and there is an inner tension in the believer that can be resolved only by reconciliation with God or radical separation from him through disbelief. The believer, as a whole human being, truly accepts the Word of God in action alone by living the Christian life, which is not a result of faith but its authentic working-out in man; in his actions, man gives his full assent to the fact that the mystery of Christ is real.[7]

---

[7] A contradiction between faith and life betrays the fact that incredulity and faith share the mind of the believer. If faith does not transform our lives, incredulity is still alive in us.

IV

FAITH: MAN'S RESPONSE TO GRACE
AND AN EXPRESSION OF THIS RESPONSE

By faith man responds to God who calls him from within
through grace, and from without through his message of salvation. The New Testament writings describe the presence of the
Spirit of Christ (the Holy Spirit, sent by the glorified Christ) in
man as an inner *illumination,* opening the hearts of men to the
Gospel;[8] as a divine attraction, making man docile to the mystery of Christ (Jn. 6, 44-46); as a *faculty of knowing,* disposing
man to communion of life with Christ through faith (1 Jn. 5,
20); as an inner experience of filial trust in God, our Father in
Christ (Rom. 8, 14-17; Gal. 4, 5-6). As exegesis recognizes
and the magisterium of the Church confirms,[9] these formulas
affirm that grace has its own repercussion on the depths of man's
consciousness and stamps a mysterious tendency toward intimacy
with God on his spiritual faculties.

The tradition that stems from St. Augustine and the Thomist
theology influenced by it have explained this illumination by
grace as the ineffable *inner Word* of God himself, which he alone
can speak and in which he reveals himself as God.[10] His call is
not concretized in any particular representation; God reveals
himself in his call as he who transcends any conceptual content.

---

[8] Acts 16, 14; 1 Cor. 1, 10; 2 Cor. 4, 4-6; Eph. 1, 17; 4, 17-19; Col. 1, 21; 3, 9-10; Mt. 11, 25; 16, 17.

[9] Cf. L. Cerfaux, *Le chrétien dans la théologie paulinienne* (Paris, 1962), pp. 243, 271-86, 465; F. Amiot, *Les idées maîtresses de S. Paul* (Paris, 1959), pp. 133-49; H. Schlier, *Der Brief an die Epheser* (Düsseldorf, 1962), pp. 72-82, 167-76; E. Schweizer, "πνεῦμα," in *Theol. Wörterb. z. N.T.* VI, pp. 428-36; M. E. Boisnard, "La connaissance de Dieu dans l'Alliance nouvelle d'après la première Epître de S. Jean," in *Rev. bibl.* 56 (1949), pp. 365-91; J. Alfaro, "Cognitio Dei et Christi in I Johannis," in *Verb. Dom.* 39 (1961), pp. 82-91; *idem, Fides, Spes, Caritas* (Rome, 1963), pp. 234-68; Vatican Council II, *Dogmatic Constitution on Divine Revelation,* n. 5, and *Dogmatic Constitution on the Church,* n. 12; Conc. Araus. II, can. 7 (Denz-Schönm., 377).

[10] Cf. B. Duroux, *La psychologie de la foi chez S. Thomas d'Aquin* (Fribourg, 1956); J. Alfaro, *Supernaturalitas fidei iuxta S. Thomam* (Rome, 1963); M. Seckler, *Instinkt und Glaubenswille nach Thomas von Aquin* (Mainz, 1961).

He communicates and manifests himself through grace, with no other mediation than his ineffable attraction toward himself, and man knows God a-conceptually in living the experience of his call. This knowledge is not a vision of God or an immediate experience of him, but the living of a tendency toward the transcendent one in himself and, in this tendency, an a-conceptual grasp of man's final end—the absolute as grace.

The inner Word of God and the outer word of the Church (which transmits the message of Christ) are mutually necessary and complementary. The illumination of grace dynamically precontains the structure of the act of faith, since it enables man to accept the Christian message as revealed by God, and thus to give conceptual expression to the mystery of God who saves him through Christ.

Without the inner Word, man could not see the expression of divine revelation in the message—that is, he could not believe in God who reveals himself in Christ. Without the doctrinal content of the message, man could not fully and humanly seize the true reality of God who saves him through Christ. The message gives human form to the same reality that man lives through the inner experience of grace—that is, the invitation to free acceptance of God's free gift of himself, communicating himself as absolute love and saving man from his limitations as a creature through participation in the life of God. The content of the Christian message gives man conceptual knowledge of the mysterious experience of what God himself works in the depths of man through Christ and his Spirit.

Divine revelation implies a personal intervention by God, calling man to participate in his life, and the expression of this intervention in the mystery of his Son made man, the mediator of all grace and all revelation. In man the grace of Christ interiorizes God's call to communion of life in the personal encounter of mutual self-giving. In the message of Christ (the personal Word of the Father, expressing himself in human words through the incarnation), God himself, Father of Christ and our Father in Christ, comes to meet us. Revelation, being the Word of God to man, implies both God's gift of himself to man and the human expression of this gift.

This dual aspect of revelation is reflected in the dual aspect of faith—man's personal response to God's inner call by entrusting himself to God, and his acceptance of the message. As a personal response, faith is man's giving of himself in filial trust and loving submission to God, in reply to the ineffable gift and manifestation of God in grace—that is, man's free entrusting of himself to the absolute as love. As the acceptance of the message of Christ, faith is the expression of man's personal response in entrusting himself to God who in Christ reveals himself and saves mankind.

Both aspects (personal-inner and doctrinal-outer) are as necessary to faith as they are to revelation. It is the vital fusion of both that constitutes the act of faith. However, each is not of equal importance. The inner-personal aspect, "believing in God", has the principal place. The primary purpose of faith, determined by God's ineffable attraction toward himself, is to enter into contact with God himself. Through faith man seeks God principally in the personal role of his self-revelation, to receive from him what he reveals of himself; this is the only way the content of revelation is accepted as the Word of God himself. We believe what God reveals because it is God who reveals it.[11]

V

DEFECTIVE EXPRESSIONS OF MAN'S
RESPONSE TO GOD IN FAITH AND ITS FULL EXPRESSION

Faith, therefore, is made whole by man's response, entrusting himself to the absolute as grace in confident submission (a response determined by God's call to intimacy with him and lived

[11] St. Thomas expressly affirms the supremacy of the personal aspect of revelation and faith (which coincides with their formal aspect: "believing God") over their doctrinal content. Cf. *Summa Theologica* II-II, q. 11, a. 1; q. 1, a. 1; q. 2, a. 2; *De Ver.*, q. 14, a. 8 in C. et ad 2. 7. 9; a. 7, ad 7; *In Joann.*, c. 6, lect. 3. This supremacy parallels the supremacy of the divine over the human in Christ, of the invisible over the visible in the Church, of the spirituality of man, which opens him to God, over his corporeality, which opens him to the world.

in the ineffable experience of God's personal self-giving in his call), and by the expression of this response in his acceptance of the doctrinal content of the Christian message, whose nucleus is precisely Christ's communication of the life of God to men. Does it follow from this that faith, absolutely necessary for salvation as man's response to the God of revelation and grace, cannot exist without its expression in acceptance of the Christian message?

Vatican Council II has produced a series of statements that shed new light on this delicate theological problem and accurately indicate its solution. (1) Each and every man is called by God to share in his divine life through association with the mystery of the cross and resurrection of Christ. This call is made through the grace of Christ, working unseen in all men's hearts, whatever the particular circumstances of their lives. (2) Every man must respond to God's call through grace with faith, without which there can be no participation in the mystery of Christ. (3) Neither non-culpable ignorance of the Christian revelation nor non-culpable lack of knowledge of God prevents man from being called through grace; if a man sincerely obeys the voice of his conscience, he is really responding to the God of grace, however deficient his conceptual knowledge of God and his revelation may be. (The very conceptual denial of the existence of God can sometimes stem from a false image of God and not in fact be a real denial of the real God.) (4) The rites and doctrines of the non-Christian religions contain sparks of truth which come from the light of Christ and can be considered as an educational aid toward the true God and a preparation for the Gospel: the first uncertain steps of man on his search for the unknown God. (5) Islam and Judaism know the revelation of God through the prophets, the same revelation that reached its culmination in Christ, in whose human words the Son of God spoke to us. (6) Christians invoke the triune God and confess Jesus Christ as savior and Lord; the Catholic Church possesses the fullness of revealed truth.[12]

[12] Vatican Council II, *Dogmatic Constitution on the Church*, nn. 13-17;

The conclusion to be drawn from these statements is that man cannot freely decide his position before God, but can only do so when the grace of Christ works in him. This means that for man there is no other God but the God of grace, the Father of our Lord Jesus Christ, and that the vocation to communion of life with God (the call of the God of grace) constitutes the deepest dimension of human existence.

In the (basically biblical) Augustinian-Thomist concept of grace as an inner illumination from God himself, man's being called to participation in the divine life implies God's a-conceptual manifestation and gift of himself as God objectivized, an ineffable communication of God in himself, not objectivized in representative content, but lived in the attraction of the transcendent toward himself. In response to this inner invitation man feels himself called to free acceptance of the absolute in his gratuitous self-giving, even though he has no reflective consciousness of this feeling.

Man's free response (acceptance or rejection), anticipated and prefigured in his experience of this divine call, includes a true choice of faith, since man really accepts or rejects God who communicates and manifests himself in his attraction toward himself. This choice does not in itself possess the human fullness proper to the act of faith, since it does not give conceptual form to divine revelation or human expression to reality, which decides the real meaning of the choice itself. From this point of view it is an incomplete act of faith which does not achieve its full human expression in affirmation of the content of revelation. But it is a choice that implies an embryonic faith, rooted in the ineffable depth of freedom—its exercise can transcend the conceptual knowledge that conditions this exercise—and not developed in the corresponding categorical expression; it is a faith that is lived, but circumscribed (by circumstances outside the control of man's will), and one which will lead to conceptual assent.

Pastoral Constitution on the Church in the Modern World, nn. 1, 3-4; *Decree on the Church's Missionary Activity*, nn. 2-3, 7; *Declaration on the Relation of the Church to Non-Christian Religions*, nn. 2-4.

Whether man knows it or not, the ultimate meaning of his existence is decided by his acceptance or rejection of the transcendent as grace—that is, by his existential posture of belief or disbelief. This posture implies intentional—not *thought* intention, but the *real* intention of human freedom shot through with grace, intention *lived* in the depths of consciousness—affirmation or negation of the God of revelation and grace. By responding to God who reveals and gives himself, man in the last analysis is tending toward Christ, since God's revelation and grace coincide with the incarnation, which in itself contains the revelation and personal self-giving of God the Father to the man Christ, his Son, and in Christ to all men.

By the very fact of being the Word made flesh, Christ is revealer and savior in whom the Father reveals and gives himself to us. All God's revelation and saving intervention in the history of man tend finally toward the supreme presence of God in history, Christ. This is why the choice of faith cannot reach a fully human expression without explicit knowledge of the revelation of Christ: only in the light of the Christian message can man fully understand himself, understand the real meaning of the decisive choice of his life.

Man's response to grace has a supernatural tendency toward God who reveals himself in Christ. This is why it really implies clinging to God in faith—"believing God". The categorical expression of his clinging (the doctrinal content, the acceptance of which brings man to realize his surrender to God through faith) will inevitably reach varying levels according to the different degrees of knowledge of God and of his revelation that each man can achieve in the historical circumstances of his existence. A man who is completely ignorant of the very existence of God, through no fault of his own, can express the basic intention of his choice in the affirmation of any absolute value (whatever its name) of which he has knowledge.

Non-Christian religions can give men insights that are a "preparation for the Gospel" and include some idea of a saving God and even of loving trust in him. Here the living choice of faith is already beginning to take on conceptual expression, and the very concepts it uses point toward Christ, in whom they are definitely realized. Judaism and Islam have inherited the Old Testament categories of revelation and grace, whose full realization is Christ. But Christianity alone allows man to entrust himself to God in faith through the acceptance of a doctrine that fully expresses the reality of salvation itself. Only in the Christian faith do man's surrender to the God of grace and the expression of this surrender in acceptance of revealed doctrine fully coincide. The inner action of the Spirit and the outer control of the hierarchical structure enable the Church to possess and infallibly transmit the content of the Christian revelation—the faith of the Christian receives its ecclesial fulfillment in the communion in faith of the whole Church.[13]

It is not difficult to understand why man receives justification *as grace through faith* (Rom. 3, 21-31; 4, 5-16) and possesses "eternal life" (Jn. 3, 16. 36). The characteristic posture of faith is precisely the posture of receiving the absolute gift—God himself. It is a posture of pure receiving and (in this pure receiving) recognizing the absolute gratuitousness of absolute love. The Christian message is a full elaboration of this posture; in it the

---

[13] The act of faith is based, under divine attraction, on the infallible truth of God itself ("believing God": the personal-inner, or "formal" aspect of faith; cf. *Summa Theologica* II-II, q. 1, a. 1; q. 5, a. 3 ad 2; *In Boet. De Trin.*, q. 2, a. 2) and tends toward God who saves us through Christ. This supernatural tendency of faith implies (vital, not conceptual, implication) the affirmation of our final salvation through Christ. This is why the act of faith is always absolutely true in its characteristic structure ("believing God") and in its orientation toward Christ, the final end of revelation, however false it may be in its partial or total concrete objective content. The measure of completeness with which the representative content expresses the mystery of Christ will determine whether the act of faith draws a man near the Church or incorporates him fully into it. Vatican Council II defined the various grades of approximation or belonging to the Church according to the various degrees of categorized expression of the Christian revelation; "preparation for the Gospel" in non-Christian religions; the announcement of Christ in Old Testament revelation; the confession of Christ as Son of God and savior in the Christian religions; full belonging to the Church in Catholicism, which possesses the fullness of Christian revelation (cf. the texts of Vatican Council II cited in footnote 12).

Church confesses the grace of God who gives us his love and through his Son sends his Spirit in order to testify in the depth of men's hearts that God is our Father (Rom. 8, 14-17). Through faith man enters here and now into communion of life with God and this communion is realized in knowledge of Christ (Jn. 17, 3; 1 Jn. 5, 20), which means clinging with one's whole self to the message and person of Christ.

Gregory Baum, O.S.A. / *Toronto, Canada*

The Magisterium in a Changing Church

One of the difficult problems of contemporary theology is to combine the indefectibility and infallibility of the ecclesiastical magisterium with the doctrinal changes that are taking place in our day. While we tend to say that the Catholic Church never changes her teaching, the benevolent observer looking at the Church from the outside is greatly impressed by the doctrinal reform initiated by Vatican Council II.

Is it possible to speak of the teaching of the Church as changing? We may divide the object of authoritative ecclesiastical teaching into three areas: (1) divine revelation and what is connected with it; (2) the natural values of human life, personal and social; (3) theological and biblical research.[1] That teaching changes in the last category is quite evident. The authoritative ecclesiastical positions in matters of scholarship have a purely pastoral purpose, and it is not surprising that the advance of science has a great influence on changing the official positions. As a typical example of an official position, binding at one time but later abandoned, one may refer to the decisions of the Biblical Commission in the early years of this century. In the second area, dealing with natural wisdom, we also find an evolution of teaching. Since man's self-understanding depends on many fac-

[1] G. Baum, "Risk and Renewal," in *The Furrow* 16 (1965), pp. 336-52.

tors, personal and social, and hence constantly develops in history, it is not surprising that the Church's position in personal and social ethics has undergone a good many changes. The classical example is the issue of religious liberty. While the ecclesiastical magisterium of the last century totally rejected the idea that religious liberty was a right of the human person,[2] Vatican Council II has formally declared that religious liberty is, in fact, an inalienable right of man and that this right must be respected by all institutions and societies.

The problem is more difficult when we come to the first area mentioned above, the *revelata* and the *cum revelatis connexa.* This is the primary area in which the Church exercises her divinely appointed teaching office. Yet even here we are unable to claim that the Church's teaching is a fixed body of truths handed on from generation to generation. Even in this area do we find growth of understanding and hence the change of certain positions. There can be no doubt that some doctrinal positions taught by the highest ecclesiastical magisterium in the past no longer express present-day teaching.

A good example is the famous dictum, *extra Ecclesiam nulla salus,* which expressed the conviction of the Church Fathers that in general there is no salvation outside of the Church.[3] In the Middle Ages this teaching was strongly endorsed by the ecclesiastical magisterium. An ecumenical council, the Council of Florence, spelled out the teaching in some detail. "[The Church] firmly believes, professes and preaches that no one outside the Catholic Church, whether pagan or Jew or heretic or schismatic, can have a share in eternal life . . . but is destined instead for

---

[2] Pius IX in *Quanta Cura:* "From this completely false conception of social rule (naturalism) they did not hesitate to foster that erroneous opinion which is especially injurious to the Catholic Church and the salvation of souls, called by our predecessor Gregory XVI *deliramentum* (insane raving), namely that freedom of conscience and of worship is the proper right of each man, and that this should be proclaimed and asserted in every rightly constituted society" (*Denz.,* 1690; also cf. 1613).

[3] J. Baumer, "Extra Ecclesiam nulla salus," in *Lexikon f. Theologie u. Kirche,* Vol. 3, cols. 1320-21.

the eternal fire prepared for the devil and his angels unless he is received into the Church before the end of his life." [4] The Council insisted that only those who belong to the Catholic Church have access to eternal salvation and even endorsed the ancient quotation: "No one can be saved, no matter how much almsgiving he does, nor even if he shed his blood in the name of Christ, unless he remains integrally united to the flock of the Catholic Church." [5]

The contemporary magisterium of Vatican Council II has retained the statement that outside the Church there is no salvation,[6] but the conciliar documents also make it quite clear that this sentence is no longer taught *eodem sensu eademque sententia*. According to the repeated teaching of Vatican Council II there is plentiful salvation outside the Church.[7] God is redemptively at work in the whole of humanity. What remains true about the ancient statement is that the redemptive action of God among men prefigures, prepares or manifests the Church.[8] Wherever grace is given, it is given in view of the Church—and in this sense there is no salvation apart from the Church.

We are forced to admit that even while the creedal formula of ecclesiastical teaching remains unchanged, a doctrinal development on the meaning of the Gospel is possible and has, in fact, taken place. Such basic questions as who are other people, what is the human person, what is the world we live in, and what is Christian life are answered differently today than they were in the past. Our doctrinal understanding of anthropology has undergone an extraordinary evolution, and for this reason our judgments on how the Church is situated in the human family and how Christians must act in this world have been profoundly

[4] *Denz.*, 714.
[5] *Ibid.*
[6] *Dogmatic Constitution on the Church*, nn. 12, 26.
[7] Cf. *Dogmatic Constitution on the Church*, nn. 15, 16; *Pastoral Constitution on the Church in the Modern World*, n. 22; *Decree on Ecumenism; Declaration on the Relation of the Church to Non-Christian Religions.*
[8] *Dogmatic Constitution on the Church*, n. 2.

modified. It would be superficial to say that a change of policy on the part of the Church—religious liberty, ecumenism, dialogue, cooperation, acknowledgment of positive values in other religions—belongs simply to the practical order. No, the change that has taken place is doctrinal. The theologian is therefore obliged to examine the indefectibility and infallibility of the ecclesiastical magisterium and face the difficult question of how it can be reconciled with the changing teaching of the Church.

The very problem seems to reverse a theological trend of the past century. After Vatican Council I, Catholic theologians greatly exaggerated the infallibility of the ecclesiastical magisterium.[9] While Vatican Council I limited papal infallibility to clearly defined moments, namely, to *ex cathedra* pronouncements, a certain theological trend after the Council tried to attribute infallibility to the ordinary magisterium of the popes. The same theological writers widened the object of the Church's infallibility. How did they do this? If one considers the primary object of infallibility to be the revealed doctrine on faith and morals, i.e., the *credenda* and *facienda* of the Gospel, and the secondary object to be the *cum revelatis connexa,* these theological writers would extend this secondary object beyond those truths that are absolutely necessary to defend the Gospel to include all theological conclusions and the areas of ethical and political philosophy. On this basis these authors were able to claim that a document such as the *Syllabus of Errors* (1864) was an infallible statement of Catholic teaching. In many a manual of theology at one time used in Catholic seminaries, the ecclesiastical magisterium had become a myth.

The task of the theologian is to clarify the Christian reality of the magisterium. We must, first of all, distinguish between the *continuous magisterium* exercised in liturgy and the preparation for it in which Christ continually teaches the local Churches, and the *intermittent magisterium* exercised by ecclesiastical decrees through which the continuous magisterium is strengthened.

[9] Cf. F. Gallati, *Wenn die Päpste sprechen* (Vienna, 1960).

I

THE CONTINUOUS MAGISTERIUM

The teacher in the Church is Jesus Christ. It is he in whom God has revealed himself and continues to reveal himself to men. Jesus is the one Word which the Father speaks; for this reason there is no new revelation after the glorification of the Son. It is through the life of the Church that Christ continues to teach people. Teaching in the Church is not simply the account of the divine self-revelation that took place many hundreds of years ago; teaching in the Church is the continuation of the divine self-revelation that took flesh in Jesus Christ. Christ is still teacher in the community, and his Spirit is still at work in the hearts of men, making them grasp, assimilate and live the message of reconciliation. The victory of Christ in death and resurrection is the assurance that God will always communicate himself in the Church as the living truth.[10]

Since the paschal mystery reveals the definitive triumph of God, we are certain that till the end of time no amount of infidelity in the Church will ever basically obscure God's self-revelation among us or substantially change or falsify the saving teaching of Jesus Christ. The difficult words in this sentence are "basically" and "substantially". It is not easy to say what these words mean precisely. The victory of God in Christ has sufficiently withdrawn the mystery of God's self-disclosure from the ambiguous area of human life so that those who seek the living Gospel and communion with God are always able to find them in the Catholic Church.

Jesus is teacher in many ways. He teaches in and through every baptized Christian. Through the baptism of faith, the Christian shares in the prophetic ministry of Jesus Christ.[11] "Christ, the great prophet, who proclaimed the kingdom of his

[10] K. Rahner, "Lehramt," in *Lexikon f. Theologie u. Kirche*, Vol. 6, cols. 884-90.

[11] *Dogmatic Constitution on the Church*, nn. 10, 12.

Father both by the testimony of his life and the power of his words, continually fulfills his prophetic office until the complete manifestation of his glory through the entire Christian people, the hierarchical ministry as well as the laity." [12] This self-communication of God in the community is not confined to formal teaching. It takes place in action and witness, in mutual assistance, in conversation and love. It takes place in the self-knowledge which comes from the interaction with others. The Gospel is handed on in the Church, not as a series of teachings but as so many ways in which the living Word addresses himself to us and enters into fellowship with us. In other words, the tradition of faith is not simply doctrinal tradition; it includes the entire life of the community. "The Church in her doctrine, life, and worship, perpetuates and transmits to all generations all that she is and all that she believes." [13] Since the Spirit is at work in the life of the Church, the Church remains the locus where Jesus Christ himself instructs his people.

It is to this living tradition of the Gospel in the Church, protected as it is by the Spirit, that Catholic teaching regarding the indefectibility and infallibility of the Church has its first and foremost application. This tradition of faith is indefectible in the sense that it will never disappear from this earth; it is called infallible in the sense that it communicates unfailingly the message of salvation. While this divinely protected tradition may historically exist in greater or lesser clarity, Christ never ceases to communicate himself in this traditioning of the Gospel. The infallibility *in credendo* and *in docendo* has here its primary application.

In an altogether special way Jesus is teacher of the Church in the celebration of God's Word. This happens through the proclamation of the Gospel in the community, the reading of and the reflection on the scriptures, the explanation and application of the revealed message in the liturgical service. Through the entire worship of the Church, God in Christ addresses himself to the

[12] *Ibid.*, n. 35.
[13] *Dogmatic Constitution on Divine Revelation*, n. 9.

Church. "Christ is present in his Word, since it is he himself who speaks when the holy scriptures are read in the Church." [14] "In the liturgy God speaks to his people and Christ is still proclaiming his Gospel." [15] "In the sacred scriptures the Father who is in heaven lovingly approaches his sons and talks to them." [16] Through the Word, God communicates himself to his people in power. The Word judges and forgives, corrects and strengthens, nourishes, directs and builds up the community. At worship, especially at the eucharistic celebration, the principal worship uniting Word and Sacrament, Christ comes to his people, lays hold of them anew in the Gospel, and by creating strong faith in them makes them more truly his faithful people. It is, therefore, at worship that Christ constantly teaches the Church.

The celebration of Word and Sacrament is exercised by an hierarchical priesthood. The bishops as successors of the apostles and their helpers, the priests, are the main celebrants of the liturgical worship. They are ministers of the Word. They proclaim the Gospel, they explain it and apply it to the needs of the present. Thanks to their sacred ministry, they have a special share in the prophetic office of Christ, a share which is different from that communicated through baptism.[17] What is this difference? The share in the prophetic office of Jesus, granted through baptism, is the primary reality in the Church; the share in the prophetic office of Christ bestowed through the sacrament of orders is a ministry or service to the prophetic mission of the entire people, making it more effective, more powerful, more intense. The teaching ministry of the hierarchical priesthood does not replace the prophetic mission of the people; it is, rather, destined to protect and promote the prophetic mission of the entire Church. Through the teaching ministry of the bishops and their priests, the whole congregation of the faithful becomes more secure, more articulate, more deeply convinced in the exercise of its prophetic office.

[14] *Constitution on the Sacred Liturgy,* n. 7.
[15] *Ibid.,* n. 33.
[16] *Dogmatic Constitution on Divine Revelation,* n. 21.
[17] *Dogmatic Constitution on the Church,* n. 25.

This ministry of the Word, exercised by the hierarchical priest-hood, is what the ecclesiastical magisterium is in its first and strongest sense. Through it Jesus fulfills his own magisterium in the Church. The ecclesiastical magisterium is exercised, above all, in the sacramental liturgy of the Church. For this reason we may call it a continuous magisterium; it is as uninterrupted as the celebration of worship in the Church. It is here that the magisterium is most powerful. It is here that the people are formed and instructed by the Word of God. The scriptures take on their deepest meaning in the context of the faithful com-munity at worship. It is here that the Gospel is applied to the concrete situation of the faithful. The ecclesiastical magiste-rium, exercised in the Spirit, is indefectible and infallible, as is, indeed, the entire worship of the Church. The scriptural words, "He who hears you hears me", find here their principal appli-cation. The many strong statements on the Church's teaching authority, repeatedly made in the Catholic tradition, have their primary verification in this continuous magisterium. The con-tinuous magisterium also includes the preparation for liturgy, especially Christian catechesis.

How is the ecclesiastical magisterium preserved in the truth of the Gospel? This is the work of the Holy Spirit. But the Spirit does not act directly in each local congregation so as to protect each one of them, singly, from misunderstanding the Gospel; the Spirit, rather, acts in the universal Church, and it is through the interaction of the many local Churches in uni-versal communion that the protection and guidance of the Spirit are available to all. We read in the *Constitution on Divine Rev-elation:* "Tradition, scripture and the ecclesiastical magisterium are, according to God's wise design, so interconnected and united that none can stand without the others, and that all effectively contribute, each in its own way, under the motion of the one Holy Spirit, to the salvation of souls." [18] There is, therefore, a constant interaction between the faith of the people (tradition), the witness of scripture, and the ministry of the Word (magiste-

---

[18] *Dogmatic Constitution on Divine Revelation*, n. 10.

rium). The infallibility of the magisterium presupposes a dynamism in which the whole Church is involved. The bishops
listen to the scriptures, they listen to the understanding of the
scriptures in the people, they examine the various doctrinal
movements in the Church, test them in the light of the scriptures, and then, after mature reflection and consultation, rely-
ing on the assistance of the Spirit, they trust that their con-
scientious decisions in the assembly will bring to light the truth
of God.

Since Jesus Christ is a living person and his self-communication takes place, not simply through doctrinal statements but
through the proclamation of the Good News in the community,
it cannot be taken for granted that the continuity of the infallible
magisterium necessarily implies the immutability of Christian
doctrine. It is certain, however, that in the history of the Church
the unity of faith was preserved because a universally acknowledged teaching authority summarized certain aspects of divine
revelation in creedal statements or doctrinal decrees.

II

THE INTERMITTENT MAGISTERIUM

From the beginning the proclamation of the Good News
contained some propositions that summed up the Christian
Gospel.[19] Creedal statements are part of the New Testament
and the earliest Christian liturgies of baptism. They were summary statements which enabled the faithful to acknowledge their
common faith in a single sentence, even if this sentence revealed its true meaning only when placed into the context of
the whole Gospel. The creedal sentences communicated the
saving truth to believers because they were able to fill out the
summary statement with the whole story of salvation which
they had learned in their catechesis and the liturgy of the
Church.

[19] O. Cullmann, *The Earliest Christian Confessions* (London, 1949).

The need for creedal formulas increased with time. As the Church grew in size and doctrinal conflicts emerged among Christians it was necessary to find more statements that summarized the Christian message and thus protected the Gospel from error and misconception. Christians were firmly convinced that the greater the universality of a teaching the more certain they could be of the assistance of the Spirit. In particular, the first four ecumenical councils, which defined the trinitarian and christological mysteries in creedal formulas, were received by the entire Church with unanimity and lasting fidelity as the normative expression of the scriptural and Catholic faith. Among ecclesiastical documents the teaching of the first four councils holds a unique position.[20]

At various moments in the history of the Church, pope and bishops found it necessary to make authoritative statements of doctrine, with varying degrees of solemnity, in order to protect the unity of faith, to settle doctrinal controversy, to direct theological thought in the Church or to attend to some other need of the Christian people. When the theological manuals speak of magisterium they usually think of this intermittent magisterium, that is, of the official teaching of pope and bishops, proposed in decrees at certain definite moments of history. Yet, since this intermittent teaching is not the first meaning of magisterium, it is impossible to obtain a theology of the magisterium by reflecting on the universal teaching of doctrine in decrees. The first meaning of magisterium is the continuous ministry of the Word, exercised by the ordained ministers in local Churches. The ecclesiastical teaching in doctrinal decrees must be understood as a special help to the continuous ministry of the Word. Doctrinal decrees never stand by themselves. They must be placed into the wider context of the teaching of the entire Gospel.

In our day some questions have arisen about the intermittent magisterium which we are not yet able to answer.

[20] Y. Congar, "La primauté des quatre premiers conciles oecumeniques," in *Le Concile et les conciles* (Paris, 1960).

According to Catholic teaching, some propositions proposed by the intermittent magisterium are infallible, i.e., they are authoritative witnesses to divine revelation, preserved from error. No future development of doctrine will ever negate the reality expressed in these propositions. They are dogma. What are these infallible statements of doctrine? They are those proposed by the solemn teaching of the Church (ecumenical councils and popes acting as supreme teachers) and by what is called the universal ordinary magisterium. The term "universal ordinary magisterium" is not clearly defined. It is usually understood as the teaching of the Catholic bishops and their Churches, dispersed throughout the world. There is good evidence, however, that this is too wide an understanding of the universal ordinary magisterium. Since each bishop teaching by himself, and his Church with him, may be led into error, it is not convincing to suggest that the collective sum of their teaching enjoys the special privilege of infallibility. Something must intervene between the dispersed teaching of the bishops and the creation of the universal ordinary magisterium. There are good arguments for saying that a doctrine becomes part of this universal ordinary magisterium only through a process of deliberation and consent among the bishops, in other words, through a collegial act on their part.[21] Such an understanding of the universal ordinary magisterium considerably reduces its content, and we are able to admit that many doctrinal positions taught in all the Churches by force of custom have, by this fact alone, no claim to infallibility.

The authoritative magisterium of the Church includes infallible and non-infallible teaching. Do we know where, precisely, the dividing line between these two areas lies? As we have mentioned, infallible teaching has to do with revelation. The ecclesiastical magisterium is infallible in proposing the revealed Gospel (primary object) and in certain situations defending and explaining it (secondary object). The secondary object has to

[21] H. Pissarek-Hudelist, "Das ordentliche Lehramt als kollegialer Akt des Bischofskollegiums," in *Gott in Welt* (Freiburg im Br., 1964).

do with issues that are *absolutely* necessary for the preservation of the Gospel. The reason for this is that a proposition is infallible, not simply because it is true but also and above all because it is a test of fidelity to the revealed Gospel.

It would seem, therefore, that the Church cannot always tell whether a particular teaching is held infallibly or not. The notion of universal ordinary magisterium is still too vague, and the object of infallibility can be circumscribed only abstractly. The Church often does not know what she knows. It is rather the actual life of the Church, the doctrinal reflection within the Church and the need to clarify certain pastoral issues, that eventually lead to a clearer realization of what the Church holds infallibly.

It is, moreover, evident from the above remarks that to understand the meaning of a defined doctrine, it must be placed in the historical context in which it was first formulated. It was at that time intended as a service to the Christian people and the contemporary ministry of the Word. Doctrinal definitions must, therefore, be related to the tradition of the Church. Such historical studies are only beginning. We have as yet no hermeneutical principles for the interpretation of the ecclesiastical magisterium. Since we do not know at this moment what the application of form criticism will do to the doctrinal statements of the past, we are often quite unable to answer the question, "What is the Church teaching on this or that subject?" even when such a subject has been treated in ecclesiastical documents.

A deeper understanding of divine revelation at the Vatican Council has made the Catholic theologian more conscious of the transcendence of God's Word over any and every expression of it in the Church. We realize that a true categorical statement we make about another person and his relationship to us is transcended by reality, so that we could and even should continue indefinitely to qualify the first statement. When this person is God revealing himself in Christ the reality immeasurably transcends the true and infallible statements made by the Church about his relationship to us. Every dogma would need an unending commentary qualifying it.

Growth in the understanding of the Gospel always involves an element of conversion.[22] It seems to me inadmissible to think of doctrinal development in the Church simply as a passage from truth to greater truth. What takes place is often also a passage from blindness to seeing. The ecclesiastical magisterium, though equipped with the gift of infallibility, is again and again led to acknowledge its blindness on certain issues, to confess that while God had spoken it had not really listened, and to avow with gratitude that the Spirit, speaking in the Church or even outside the Church, brought the understanding of what God had revealed from the beginning. It seems to me that this is verified in the doctrinal development of our day, when the Spirit has led the Church to an understanding of who other people are and to the realization that God is redemptively at work in the human family. We cannot speak here of a doctrinal evolution from truth to greater truth; we have to admit that God led us from blindness to sight. What was demanded was conversion. For this reason, issues such as ecumenism, the attitude to other religions and religious liberty provoked a vehement conflict at Vatican Council II. Prior to the Council the theologians who proposed the new doctrines were often exposed to pressures and censorship by the ecclesiastical magisterium.[23] To belittle the change of heart implicit in the present doctrinal development would be to overlook the suffering of these great men and prophets in the Church. How much will the conversions to which the Spirit will lead us in the future modify our teaching?

There are then three questions in regard to the intermittent magisterium which we are not able to answer. Where is the dividing line between infallible and non-infallible teaching of the Church? What is the precise meaning of defined teaching in its

[22] G. Baum, "Doctrinal Renewal," in *Journal of Ecumenical Studies* 2 (1965), pp. 377-78.

[23] Y. Congar, *Chrétiens en dialogue* (Paris, 1964), pp. xxxix-lvi.

historical context? How far will greater fidelity to the Gospel qualify present teaching? Because he cannot answer these questions the Catholic theologian of today finds it difficult to estimate the degree to which he is bound by the various ecclesiastical documents of the past. He firmly believes that Christ is constantly teaching his Church through baptized Christians and especially through the continuous ministry of the Word, exercised by the hierarchical priesthood in apostolic succession. It is the intermittent magisterium of the past that poses problems he cannot at this moment solve. The Catholic theologian of today is, therefore, willing tentatively to engage in theological inquiries even if some of his conclusions do not agree with the apparent meaning of past conciliar statements or papal encyclicals. He has witnessed how Vatican II has gone beyond many doctrinal positions, some ancient and some more recent, proposed by the ecclesiastical magisterium. At the same time the Catholic theologian wants to remain in union with the Catholic Church. He wants to be faithful to the magisterium. He realizes that wisdom is given by God to the community. As we are dependent on others for love, so we are dependent on others for truth. For this reason, the Catholic theologian has learned to profess his positions in a tentative way, as questions, as contributions to dialogue, and he refuses to engage himself wholeheartedly in his own convictions unless he knows himself to be accompanied by the brethren, that is, the Church.

Since the Church is surrounded by a climate of opinion that favors relativism in truth and values, one of her principal tasks is to defend the unchanging Gospel in a world of flux. "Jesus Christ, the same yesterday, today and tomorrow." But do the definitive character of revelation and the infallibility of the magisterium imply the immutability of dogma? The spontaneous Catholic response is to insist on the unchanging character of truth. The Church's doctrine solemnly defined can never change. At the same time the Catholic theologian must be open to the possibility that in a new historical situation the repetition of an ancient creedal formula may in fact not communicate the same truth. Could it happen that the permanence of the creedal formula does not really protect the unchanging character of revealed truth? The Catholic theologian must seriously consider the question whether the Church may find herself in a situation where she must change the formulation of her doctrine in order to announce the unchanging Gospel infallibly and defend the immutable character of divine truth.

III

NEW WAYS OF THE MAGISTERIUM

Since the ecclesiastical magisterium is a gift of Christ to the Church, the Christian people are the losers whenever the influence and authority of this magisterium weaken in the Church. The Gospel is always threatened in this world. Even the continuous magisterium, exercised in the local liturgy, is in need of correctives supplied by the Spirit through the scriptures, through the community, and also through a more universal ecclesiastical authority.

We must ask the question whether the present exercise of the universal magisterium protects the Gospel in the most effective manner. We have become aware that the Gospel is not only threatened by the unwillingness to follow the preaching of the Church, but also by the willingness to believe too much, by credulity, by myth-making present in the human heart. The Gospel may be given certain accents and put into a system of teaching so that the message communicated to those who listen is no longer the Good News of salvation but, rather, a myth of human making. Without formally denying it, the *fides catholica* can be made part of a religious system in which it is stripped of its saving power. It would be possible, for instance, to make the Gospel appear as part of a set of doctrines according to which God is a heavenly judge before whom man must strive for justification by personal effort. Grace, in such a system, would supply man with the will power to do the things he is expected to do.

The strange views which many men outside the Church have of Catholic teaching, are often drawn from the mythical understanding which Catholic people have of the Christian Gospel.

The function of the magisterium is to protect the Gospel against myth. This happens above all in the liturgy, where the scriptures are announced and applied to the needs of the present. But this should also happen through the ecclesiastical magisterium's teaching in decrees. Pope and bishops should make the Christian people conscious of the human tendency to make myths and teach them to reject the rationalizations they may make to justify the *status quo* or to defend their illness.

In this connection we must ask the uncomfortable question whether the ecclesiastical magisterium, exercised as it is by the governing body in the Church, can be totally free from the tendency to produce myths. Is not every institution tempted to create a set of doctrines (an ideology) that will protect the institution and strengthen its government? We have mentioned above the theological trend to exaggerate the infallibility granted to the Church and thus to create a mythical understanding of the Church's teaching office. This myth of the omniscient Church, created by theologians, was never endorsed in ecclesiastical documents, but neither did these documents warn the Christian people of excessive credulity or encourage them to retain their critical spirit.

Must we not admit that the negative teaching of the ancient Church on the salvational situation of men beyond her visible boundaries had strong ideological overtones? It protected the institution by insisting that without it, divine grace was not available. How are we to understand the doctrinal emphasis in a certain kind of Catholic literature, often encouraged by those in authority, even if not fully endorsed as official teaching, on the prerogatives and powers of the hierarchy and the primary role of ecclesiastical obedience in the Christian life? While a Catholic will not deny the roots of these doctrines in divine revelation, he may see in the effort to emphasize them as primary and central an ideological intention to protect the authority of the governing body.

It seems to me that it is necessary for the universal magisterium to acknowledge the reality of an ideological trend, at least as a permanent temptation. Only through such an acknowledgment will the ecclesiastical magisterium realize that it must constantly listen to God's Word in the scriptures and be open to the Spirit speaking in the people. It does not belittle the normative character of the universal magisterium to insist that for the sake of exercising its supreme function, it must always be in dialogue with the entire Church.

The deeper understanding of the pilgrim character of the indefectible magisterium would seem to demand a new way of teaching. One could imagine that the intermittent magisterium in our day might promote and protect the Gospel more effectively by raising the significant questions about it, by warning of the one-sided attempts to solve them, and by pointing out the direction in which the answers will have to be found. Pope Paul's encyclical *Ecclesiam suam* (1964) is a remarkable example of a new approach to the universal magisterium. Here the pope formulates the questions of the contemporary Church, he suggests lines of thought along which the whole community must seek the answer, and he encourages the reflection of all Christians and the research of theologians. By urging the Christian people to listen to God's Word in the scriptures, in the life of the Church and even in history, the pope leads them to transcend whatever mythical elements they may have produced for themselves, to reach out for a new obedience to the Gospel.

The pastoral needs of the Church demand that the ecclesiastical magisterium, through whom Christ guides his Church, find ways of presenting and defending the Gospel that are adapted to the needs of the contemporary Church and open to the guidance which the Spirit supplies to the people of the Lord.

Hans Urs von Balthasar/ *Basle, Switzerland*

Truth and Life

In the Old Testament God's "truth" is a concept dealing primarily with behavior, and only indirectly with essence. It is the reliability of God's pledge, of his promise; it includes both his directives for man's conduct before him and his threats which, in their own way, confirm the truth of his promise. God defines his ineffable, sovereign makeup solely by characterizing his action as reliable. Any action of his is *ipso facto* utter reliability—so much so that any oppressed person can lodge an appeal directly with God by making explicit reference to the reliability and fidelity of his dealings.

In Jesus Christ we find something more than just the fulfillment of God's promise (for that would simply mean that the account was closed). In reality, however, the fulfillment of God's relationship to man is simultaneously the unexpected revelation of God's essence. The Word that becomes flesh and dwells among us is not only "God with us"; in the spoken Word, the speaker himself steps on the scene. The Word is "God with God", the "only-begotten of the Father", who "comes into the world" and lets "his glory be seen", "full of grace and truth" (Jn. 1, 14). His glory is no longer without form (Deut. 4, 12); instead —as Ezekiel foresaw it (Ezek. 1, 26)—in the human form of the Word it shines forth as that which is above all forms. It shines forth as the eternal love of Father and Son in the Spirit,

85

gratuitously revealed to us so that it comes to be God's promise as "grace" and therefore "truth"; and now truth is not only the reliability of God's dealings but also the disclosure of God's being.

From the standpoint of the history of ideas, this means that John fulfills the Old Testament concept of truth so completely, both within and beyond itself, that the Greek concept of truth also appears completely fulfilled within and beyond itself. It is the manifestation of being itself in the being who appears before us. In theological terms, it means that God no longer conceals his unfathomable makeup behind his pattern of conduct; instead, in the Trinity of the salvation-economy—the Trinity which crosses over to us—the immanent Trinity is laid open to us and offered for our participation.

God Creates Truth in the Human Realm

In the realm of men, fidelity is often shattered and always threatened. God's unbroken fidelity can permeate this realm only in the form of judgment, of ever continuing evaluation and weeding out. This weeding out becomes all the more inexorable as God's fidelity permeates further. It calls for the rejection of the whole unresponsive nation, so that the "holy remnant" might be won over precisely through catastrophe. This remnant manages to recognize God's thunderbolt as the final revelation of his truth and fidelity, and to accept the blow as vicarious atonement. By complete submission to the judgment event, the "holy remnant" becomes an active participant.

Here the Old Testament possibility for man is completely fulfilled: to roam through the realm of divine fidelity that has been opened up to him; to make God's truth the law of his existence; "to do what is truth" (cf. 2 Chr. 31, 20), "to walk in truth" (Ps. 26, 3) and to be a "man of truth" (Exod. 18, 21; Neh. 7, 2). The ultimate basis for doing this is an act whereby man acknowledges God's truth, takes it at face value and adopts it as his own—the act of faith.

Jesus Christ is the intrinsic fulfillment of this act. He fully carries out the judicial evaluation and weeding out involved in God's Word, even to the point of being both the judger and the judged, and thus he surpasses and perfects the role of representative first assumed by the "Ebed Yahweh". He descends into the deepest recesses of darkness, and is not overcome (Jn. 1, 5). As the embodiment (incarnation) of God's full truth, he fully works it out and lets it work fully on him. He shows God's people the love shining through God's fidelity; as a result, God appears as the absolute and essential love. His "for us" is perfected in Christ's "among us" and "in us"; in this way God's "in himself" is revealed. His perfect human response to the mandate of the Father is the revelation of the Father's love for his only-begotten Son (in whom the Old Covenant is now fulfilled and dissolved); it is the revelation of the Son's love for the Father (in which totally submissive faith, total existence *in* truth, is caught up into existence *as* truth). The obedience of the perfect creature becomes the expression of trinitarian love, and it receives this as its intrinsic form.

This is perfectly fulfilled in the mystery of the "Spirit of truth" (Jn. 14, 17; 16, 13). Because the Son enters the finality of judgment and breathes forth his Spirit back to the Father, the Spirit pulsing between Father and Son is set free to the world. To the world at large he bears witness to the love of Father and Son: subjectively, in that he is this love; objectively, in that he represents it, establishes it and declares it—even in the face of a world that does not yet believe.

It is only in this objective aspect of the Spirit that an analogy with "theoretical" truth becomes feasible in the biblical-ecclesial sphere. But this theoretical element is not opposed to the "existential"; it is but a *function* of the existential. It is convincing evidence that God's absolute fidelity-love has been fully realized in Christ. In the subjective testimony of the Spirit, this evidence is

the truth itself—set forth, put to work and made operative in
everyone who "accepts" the testimony of the Spirit.

The Theoretical Structure of Truth
Enmeshed in the Biblical-Existential

The events of revelation and of faith cannot take place independently, running a separate course parallel to the events
involving natural knowledge. Revelation must be a process
whereby the object revealing itself elevates the natural knowledge process above and beyond itself and moves it toward a
still unattained perfection (*visio*).

Natural knowledge is sparked by a mystery—the difference
between the individual thing and being as a whole, when they
are objects of knowledge. In this capacity the individual thing
shows up as belonging to the realm of being as a whole, while
being as a whole can only be encountered when it has endured
the humiliation and alienation of being encapsuled in individual
entities. When it undergoes this latter transformation, being is
lit up. It shows up as a mysterious reality, as self-giving, as the
good (Plato, Plotinus); but at the same time it withdraws and
hides itself because it cannot point clearly to itself from within
any existing being.

This mystery is accessible to the knowing mind. From a pre-
awareness of being in general, it can apprehend concrete individual realities as such and recognize their relationship to
being. But it is always and only particular, tangible realities that
can be set within the horizon of being. Within this horizon the
object is first presented to me as something that is (or is not):
verum. Thus it later may come to strike me as something to be
taken seriously by me: *bonum*.

The revelation of the living God in Christ lights up anew the
horizon of being. In the being who emerges (Christ), the horizon
of being moves closer to us—although in other respects it moves
away from us. Moreover, the way in which it moves toward us

in Christ makes it recognizable as pure and absolute self-giving. Precisely because God, as Trinity, is self-giving, he does not need to drain off his being into other beings in order to be himself; his humiliation in Christ is free and gratuitous. This means that his truthfulness—which is part of his very being, which in the salvation-economy reveals his bedrock love and reaches its culmination in Christ—is itself the absolute, unsurpassable *good*. And it does not first need to be set out at a distance, as an object for abstract (theoretical) contemplation.

Thus, when man looks forward to receiving God's revelation, his anticipation must be something more than open-ended neutrality toward every possible being. It must embody the presupposition that everything transmitted in God's revelation (intelligible or not) is *a priori* truth-goodness; this precisely is *faith*. Whatever the self-illuminating bedrock of love intends for me by his act of revelation in Christ, every attempt to contemplate this action from a distance presupposes that an act of eternal love has already done its work on me. Moreover, my contemplation (based on faith), whereby I freely decide to let this action be true for me, is necessarily produced with the cooperation of God's eternal love.

Faith is a gift from the Holy Spirit of revelation. He infuses into me the act which God has performed for me. In doing this, he exercises both his subjective and objective function—because it is, after all, an action of God. Subjectively, the Holy Spirit connaturalizes my person (subject) to the love of the Father in the Son (through faith, hope and charity). Objectively, the Holy Spirit fashions the objective forms of testimony which bear witness to God's objective action (historical revelation, Church, scripture, tradition, dogma); he also shapes them to match my propensity for belief. The objective forms which the testimony assumes only *seem* to be "theoretical truth". In reality they are a concrete expression of the love done for me. Objectively I am enmeshed in this love; subjectively I am called to *realize* what is in fact *already real*.

God's act of love for the world, embodied in Christ, is already *performed;* it is a fully accomplished fact. Now it must become fully *accepted* as such (in the Holy Spirit). It must become fully accepted and embodied in the Church so that the Church becomes his immaculate bride, without spot or taint, as is already the case in Mary (Sion, Ecclesia, Uxor Agni). The believing Christian, therefore, insofar as he can, must bring his existence into conformity with the range of eternal love revealed in Christ. Just as the commandments (Torah) of the Old Testament were the concrete revelation of promised grace—which men were to follow—so the objective mental outlook of the Church (scripture and dogma) is the objective articulation of grace fully revealed and actualized.

The Freedom of the Spirit

The Spirit breathes where he wills. Once again he is a great freedom, proceeding from the love between Father and Son. However, he will not forget where he has come from. His whole freedom will consist in testifying over and over again, in the most unpredictable ways, to the love of Father and Son. "He will not speak on his own authority, but whatever he hears he will speak. . . . He will glorify me, for he will take what is mine and declare it to you" (Jn. 16, 13-14). In this tension lies the mystery of the revelation of the Spirit, and hence of the Church too—for every age, ours included.

The Spirit has formed the Church, displaying absolute fidelity to Christ's revelation and exercising his absolute freedom to interpret it. He is the Spirit of dogma, and the propositions of dogma are true insofar as they are a function and an expression of the Church's understanding of the Christ-mystery, as given to it by the Holy Spirit. They cannot be taken out of this setting; therefore, they do not have any *purely* theoretical (i.e., non-experiential, non-existential) truth. To the extent that the Church is docile to the Spirit, it can—as the shepherd of Christendom and of all mankind—exercise its freedom to rethink and reformulate the Christ-mystery for each new age.

In all this, of course, the Church must remember that, however unfathomable and sovereign the Spirit's freedom may be, it is the freedom of that Spirit which pulses between the Father and the Son-made-man. If the Church remains aware of its mission from Christ, then it has only one guiding norm in addressing itself to a new age: the Holy Spirit, the Lord of all alterations in the Christian message.

Hence there cannot be any essential (dogmatic) difference between a "dogmatic" statement and a "pastoral" statement made by the Church's magisterium. It cannot lie in the difference between theoretical truth and practical-existential truth. From all that has been said, it is apparent that such a difference can no more exist in the Church of Christ than it can in the Holy Spirit, who is objective witness only because he is subjective fulfillment; than it can in Jesus Christ, who is the representation of God's triune truth only because he displayed his love by being obedient unto death; than it can in God himself, who is truth precisely because he is the manifestation of absolute, mutual self-giving. For the Church there is no form of truth except that fashioned by Christ. That particular form of truth has enmeshed the human (philosophical) form of truth within itself, so that the human form can no longer make any separate claims. In doing this, it has saved and elevated man's truth.

Nor can the difference between "dogmatic" and "pastoral" be based on the fact that a dogmatic statement relies more on scripture for its concepts and vocabulary, while a pastoral statement relies more on the concepts and vocabulary of mankind today. Every dogmatic formulation by the Church is also, of necessity, an expression of its pastoral love, just as the truth of Christ's Person and Word was always an expression of God's pastoral care (consider the parables, for example). Every dogmatic formulation must be interpreted in this way. It can never be oriented toward a *purely theoretical* truth, which simply does not

exist from a Christian standpoint. On the other hand, every
fully authoritative statement of the Church—even if this statement is called "pastoral"—can only spring from the Church's
mission to truth, and this mission cannot be separated in the
slightest degree from the Church's pastoral mission.

In their conceptual formulation, their thought-content and
their manner of presentation, such pastoral statements are free
and fresh alterations produced by the Holy Spirit who inspires
the Church. We therefore have *the right, and indeed the grave
duty, to interpret these formulations from within the heart of
biblical revelation.* The profound layers of truth buried within
revelation are evidently also susceptible to this interpretation
because the Church speaks with authority.

We Christians had not given enough thought to the fact that
God's emphatic "Yes", as uttered by Christ (2 Cor. 1, 19), is
an expression of the triune God's fidelity and love toward his
entire creation, toward the Father's original creation which must
be led, through reconciliation in Christ, to fulfillment in the
Spirit. We had not given enough thought to the fact that all the
potentialities for good inherent in this creation have been assumed into Christ and therefore have been entrusted to the
Church's dogmatic and pastoral attention and care. Hence, if
the theologian is interpreting conciliar documents and fails to
find the dogmatic—or, better, the revelational—background of
a pastoral statement expressed clearly or fully enough, then he
has the right and the duty to *fill this out and thus make it visible.*
Why? Because *a priori* it must exist.

There can only be slight shifts of emphasis between the two
aspects, corresponding to the two (always unified) aspects of the
Holy Spirit's activity: to faithfully preserve Christ's revelation,
and to translate it freely into all human modes of thought. Something "pastoral", which was not fully covered dogmatically,
would not live up to the original mandate: "Feed my sheep."

If the pastoral authority reflects on the basic function of the
Holy Spirit, it must always come to focus on the full-blown concept of the Church where the ever concrete and actualized truth

of Christ's revelation finds full and concrete acceptance, leaving no abstract or theoretical loose ends. In short, the pastoral authority must focus on the *Church of the saints,* which comprises the complete concept—hence, the canon—of ecclesial existence. The canon of holiness, however, is not left to the arbitrary invention and legislation of Christians. In every age the Holy Spirit bestows it upon the Church, often in unexpected ways. Here the necessary alterations proceed from the center.

Marie-Dominique Chenu, O.P./*Paris, France*

Theology as an Ecclesial Science

The theologian, *theo-logos,* is literally he who speaks the Word of God, and since God speaks his Word in human terms, the theologian also speaks the Word of God in human terms. Moreover, since God speaks his Word to a people, to a "Church", the theologian speaks the Word of God in a Church, in the ecclesial community.

In its fundamental homogeneity, such is the economy of a revelation which from start to finish is enunciated, developed, built up and propagated according to the laws and behavior of its *subject:* man—man viewed both individually and collectively, as an act of testimony, in accordance with the existential relationship of a communion with God revealing itself in the history of humanity. Never, on pain of death, must *theology* part company with *faith* which sets it in motion and puts the seal on its achievements. The avatars of the very word *theology*—whose history in the Christian era, and even before that in the pagan era, tells us so much—find their true conceptual, doctrinal and scientific form in Christianity only in the light of faith and of the decision it implies.

Thus, whatever formal distinctions can be made in the last analysis, this lofty and symbolical nominal definition does not lead us away from the elemental power of its etymology; *theologia*—even if it becomes, for the sake of argument, a branch of "learning" in the specific sense—is the Word of God; theology, as a mode of understanding, is still faith. Even though we must now, in accordance with the theme of this volume of *Concilium,* analyze in itself the scientific and argumentative function of theology, it is important to preserve its psychological and epistemological continuity with the preceding studies dealing with revelation, faith, dogma and the truth of God in himself and in man. History teaches us that the ruptures in this homogeneous tissue have simultaneously dehumanized faith, desacralized theology, rationalized mystery, withered pastoral charity and dishonored the Word of God in the eyes of men.

I

THEOLOGIANS AT THE COUNCIL

Let us pose the problem in the present circumstances—which certainly constitute a particularly favorable moment, with the Church, guided by the principles of the past Council, in the process of understanding its faith in the context of the present-day world. For theology does not subsist in written treatises alone, but in the whole Church taking conscious stock of the Word of God entrusted to it.

We do not claim to establish a theological method on the basis of this operation, solemn though it is; reflective induction must be based on the whole history of the Church, on all the phases of its theological work from the earliest days onward. But the major episode of a council, and of this council in particular, is rich in meaning. It has in any case been subtended, consciously and unconsciously, by four centuries of Counter-Reformation work, by the acute thought provoked since the beginning of the 20th century by the introduction of the critical disciplines into the world of theology, and, finally, by the recent opposition offered by a certain kind of Scholasticism living on itself far from its sources and the concrete existence of the Church.

This had direct repercussions at the Council where, during the first session, a lively reaction made itself apparent in the criticisms of the preconciliar schemas which had been elaborated in the atmosphere of this Scholasticism. It was the influence of this complex that gave rise for a moment to the ambiguous distinction—swiftly eliminated—between "doctrinal" and "pastoral", which, in its most obdurate form, came precisely from an unbalanced conception of theology, to the detriment of the existential truth of the faith and of the functional unity of theology in its component parts. Basically it was the subject of theology and faith itself, which was the issue at stake. Mindful of the vistas opened up by John XXIII, several members made the point that the Council's aim was not so much to revise declarations, true as these might be, but to bear witness to the person of Christ, the Word of God incarnate, living today in his body which is the Church.

Only the bishops and superiors of religious orders were members of the Council by right, as makers and promulgators of the proclamations and decisions. The theologians were called as official or semi-official experts to assist in the elaboration of the problems posed and the solutions presented to the Council. Thus, the two constitutional charismata—that of apostolic witness to the faith by way of magisterial decree and that of theological science—were institutionalized at the top. Moreover, the experts were not always clerics; among them were a certain number of lay people—men, women, lobbyists—whose role as qualified consultants has been increasing in the appropriate fields. There was even one lay theologian officially appointed by his bishop —some small evidence of a very opportune presence, if it is true that theology is not in itself clerical by nature.

In the normal course of his life—on the level of thought as well as in his actions, including directives concerning moral conduct or apostolic inspirations—the bishop needs the technical assistance of the theologian. But this assistance stands out and acquires even greater value at the solemn moments when the faith has to be proclaimed and defined, not only against error but in all its density, to make its presence felt in the world. At the Council, even more than in his normal pastoral work, the bishop takes the responsibility for his decisions; the theologian is his source of information, his researcher, his advisor, even the drafter of his public or private statements. He not only provides the requisite details, but also ensures the balance of different elements in an economy in which the correct placing of truths and facts is the guarantee of orthodoxy. Thus, the theologian has no authority, as some people humorously recall; he, too, is simply one of the faithful, even if his faith is adult in the degree of information and reflection on which it is based.

The assistance provided by the theologian operated in a far larger ecclesiastical field at Vatican Council II, for Vatican Council II was not primarily a Council concerned with defining error, but expressly, in accordance with the inspiration of John XXIII, an assembly summoned to take stock of the Church's mission in a world which, by its profound mutation of the human condition, calls in question the very existence of the Church. It was not a question of juridico-dogmatic elaboration but of an inward understanding of the Word of God so as to bear witness even beyond the frontiers of Christendom. Thus the bishop, the episcopal body and the Council are not so much the magisterial organ of definition as the qualified witness proclaiming the evangelical message at a solemn moment in time.

Precisely because of this situation the theologian, without detriment to his function as expert advisor to those who exercise the magisterium, has a more penetrating role and one in greater conformity with the total function of his knowledge in the ecclesial community. Insofar as theology, rooted in faith, spontaneously or scientifically sets in motion the multiple resources of the mind to elaborate and make manifest the mystery and mysteries, it finds satisfaction, in a Church occupied in bearing witness at the Council, in nourishing with understanding —which is at the same time a charisma and a gift of the Holy Spirit—the learned or popular expressions of the faith. In fact, if we look at the work that went on at the Council—at its official

sessions as well as in its commissions, and even at the innumerable preconciliar meetings—we can see that theologians played
a large and effective part in it, especially when they had to cat-
alyze the problems and hopes—and disputes—of the world. This
was almost certainly something new in the sociological history
of councils. It was also an outstanding piece of work on the part
of theology. Let us see what its tenor was.

As soon as a subject was put on the agenda—and even, one
might say, when the agenda was being prepared at the stage of
preliminary plans—it was the theologian's official and professional task to establish the *state* of the problem. This not only
meant producing a "state of the question" in the form of an
analytical inventory of the factors concerned and a summary
of opinions, but it also involved discerning the internal motives
for inquiry into the faith, including those at work in the public
opinion of the "People of God". Indeed, it was almost certainly
this context that determined the direction of the debates. Thus,
in the case of the *Constitution on Divine Revelation,* the work
of the Council found its center of gravity when discussion moved
from the preparatory schema drawn up on the accepted or rejected hypothesis of the two sources to the more radical position
of the unity of the Word of God throughout its various modes of
transmission. At the end of a long debate the reporter expressly
made the controversy about the two sources marginal and determined the proper field of the conciliar decision. This was a matter of theological knowledge, not of Scholastic controversy. Similarly, with the *Declaration on Religious Freedom,* the first long
stage of preparation consisted of determining the precise direction of the inquiry—namely, into the public conditions of religious freedom and not into a theoretical definition of freedom.
It is well known that the state of a problem governs its solution,
not so much in its material content as in its formal object. In
any case, it all helps to rid the debate and the faith itself of overtones that compromise its purity.

The theologians' second intervention was concerned with elab-
orating a vision of the world reflecting the light of the faith.

Without losing its transcendence, faith, from the mere fact that
it is the faith in the mind of a man, implies a certain vision of
the world, a certain conception of man, a definition of society, a
philosophy of civilization, a theory of time and history, etc. People have spoken, not without some ambiguity, of "Christian philosophy". But whatever terms may be used it is clear that the
believer includes in his faith, even at the price of a certain relativism, an anthropology and even a cosmology, to the extent that
man must define his position in the world. On this subject the
Council has provided us with a most instructive experiment in
the determination of the coherence between the construction of
the world and the advent of the kingdom of God, between the
creation and the redemptive incarnation. Such was the genesis of
the famous Schema XIII, which forms a splendid illustration of
the specific role of the theologian in the history of theology as
well as in the history of councils. Thus the *Pastoral Constitution
on the Church in the Modern World* includes in its terms of
reference an introduction forming a sociological analysis of the
human condition and of the evolution of the world. Some people
objected that this was not one of the Council's tasks; in fact,
allowing for the relativity implicit in such an aim, the analysis of
the "signs of the times" is both an evangelical and theological
activity on the part of the believer and of the community of
believers, concerned as they are to bear witness to the faith in
the world.

The third activity of the theologian at the Council was concerned with the elaboration of the concepts and terms employed
to enunciate the Word of God which must be proclaimed in a
clear and fruitful way. The words themselves, on the most ele-
mentary level, demand grammatical, etymological, psychological
and historical treatment, as well as reference to contexts of
every kind and a subtle perception of the *aura* that gives them
their most secret power. It is up to the theologian, with his
exegetical equipment, to define the content of these terms which
will be employed by the bishop and the pastor, starting with the
basic Gospel terms—covenant, kingdom, sacrifice, grace, wis-

dom, mystery and so on. The theologian is a "philologian" in love with words, even before their apostolic use—words in which the message of the Gospel will be clothed today because of its present human truth.

Rarely has a council created so many words as Vatican Council II, not in the sense of creating them *ex nihilo* but in that of introducing into the official, professional language of ecclesial faith terms borrowed from the vocabulary of the secular disciplines. Thus there has appeared in the public documents of the Church a whole family of words expressing the realities of collective life in an industrial civilization. *Socializatio,* which had not occurred in the encyclical *Mater et Magistra,* categorical though this was in its description of the fact denoted by the word, is henceforth inscribed (although several members of the Council were suspicious of it) in the analysis of the human condition. With it comes the vocabulary of collective sociology, including the term "human community" (*Pastoral Constitution on the Church in the Modern World*). It is worth noting that, on the advice of the experts, the phrase "social doctrine" has been excluded. The words *communio, communitas* and their derivatives, as applied to the Church, have acquired their full significance as opposed to the juridical terms, to the extent that understanding of the mystery prevailed over the analysis of structures. Another series of words now accepted is the set of terms describing the realities of history—*historia, evolutio, progressus, dynamismus,* etc.—which were needed to denote the changing world, the evolution of humanity, the requirements of the layman in the world and the law of the Christian economy itself. Finally, in the classical terminology of dogmatic theology, the exegetical experts, in accordance with the underlying current of the Council, secured the victory of biblical language, which makes the canonical or Scholastic terms "sound sterile", as one observer put it. Thus it will be noted that the concrete expressions of scripture have been preferred to the *natura-gratia* contrast, well-founded though this phrase is on theological analysis.

Another specific field in which theologians worked during

the Council was in distinguishing causes, so as to secure a proper understanding of the human and divine realities it wished to define. The clearest case is that of atheism. Right at the start of the debate, in a decisive speech, Bishop Guerra, auxiliary bishop of Madrid, declared that it was not a question of uttering an abstract and generic condemnation of atheism, but of recognizing the causes that explain its genesis.

On the other hand, in several cases the Council did not wish to embark on an inquiry into causes—the characteristic activity of science, as Aristotle said—which would have led the Council away from bearing evangelical witness to recording rational explanations in the fields of theology and science. Here we meet again the classical distinction—part of the discipline of theology —between the promulgation of the faith by the Church in council and the theological science in which the magisterium does not have to adopt a position, insofar as orthodoxy is concerned, either on rational elaborations and differing opinions or on systematic constructions. This frontier is in fact fairly mobile but it is a constitutive one both for the transcendence of the Word of God and for the freedom of theology in its "questions".

The docility of the theologian does not resolve itself into the kind of obedience that would be willing to bend the observations, analyses and reasoning of his science in accordance with the will of authority. Theology has its laws which even the best-intentioned opportunism is not permitted to transgress. It is true that these laws only hold good within the rule of faith, and it can happen that obscure tensions block the spontaneous agreement desired on both sides. Anyone who envisaged the content of the divine mystery and the human reality to which it is communicated as a kind of mathematics would be in for a surprise. This would be a doubly false intellectualism, against which both the nature of theology and its history protest. History is full of lessons, the first of which is that a delicate understanding of faith and its data demand patient discretion. Richard Simon, who did not always possess it in his dealings with Bishop Bossuet, remains an amazing precursor of biblical criticism. In his opposition to abuses in the occupation of the new lands and the political methods used in the evangelization of the Indies, Vitoria resisted, from his chair at Salamanca, the high clerical officials who were as disloyal to natural law as to the Gospel. The apostolic theology of Lacordaire magnanimously preserved its freedom from bishoprics overtaken by events. At Vatican Council II, Bishop Pellegrino, archbishop of Turin, in demanding freedom of research in theology as elsewhere, called to mind that he had met a theologian "in involuntary exile because he had expressed opinions which we rejoice to read today in the pontifical and conciliar documents. We all know that his case is not unique".

Despite these misunderstandings the theologian remains the "technical assistant", to use the term currently used in other fields; he is *at the service* of the episcopate throughout the whole range of its magisterial and apostolic functions: scriptural teaching, sense of tradition, feeling the pulse of the Church as the organ of faith and the dwelling of the Spirit and as an organized, living community. There is no institutional or intellectual formalism here, but active participation in a concrete field, a real "place" of reflection for the theologian. To cite one of many examples, there is the domain of missionary theology which, under the law of doctrinal and practical fidelity to the episcopate, sees the deployment of the complementary charismata which the theologian carries to their necessary level of *intellectus fidei*. The episcopate draws from this a renewal of its collegial consciousness in the one and catholic Church.

II

THE THEOLOGICAL SCIENCE

Thus the conduct of Vatican Council II provides an excellent illustration of the classical thesis, *de necessitate theologiae,* an illustration that is necessarily all the more significant in that this Council gave more importance in its aims to the witness of the Gospel in the present-day world than to the discussion and refutation of errors. This enables us to define the field of theology, of the theological "science", which does not restrict itself to expedient apologetics, Scholastic lucubrations, "conclusions" deduced from the data of revelation or opinions of varying degrees of probability. It is really an *understanding of the faith,* a *speculative* and *practical* understanding, in the sense that these two terms possessed in medieval terminology. As opposed to a purely empirical pastoral attitude, a summary supernaturalism, a short-winded exegetical positivism or a false dogmatism, theological learning with its own laws is a vital necessity for the Church as the People of God, enabling it to breathe in the world.

In the light of the exceptional experience of the Council it is also possible to arrive at a better understanding and a clearer illustration of the laws, methods, structures and dynamism of this theology. Let us quickly recapitulate them.

Let us justify, first of all, the term theological *science,* obviously not in the modern sense of an experimental, positive discipline dealing with the phenomena of nature, but in the sense— Aristotelian in origin—of a rational, organic knowledge of a given fact within the framework of the believer's specific allegiance. Clearly, the rational mechanisms of "science" will not be transferred, just as they are, to the study of the mystery of God, but we must feel confidence and pleasure in allowing the intelligence to live its natural life within the framework of the assent of faith. Let us therefore hold the view that this intellectual reflection, this "cogitation" (St. Augustine, St. Thomas), practiced within the framework of this assent according to the natural laws of the mind, has its function, its autonomy, its validity in the "connaturality" of the faith, but beyond the personal and emotional experiences of this faith. This is a criterion to follow on the double plane of intellectual activity and objectivity.

It can thus be seen that all the resources of the human mind will be deployed, in the whole psychological and epistemological range of its nature, in an intelligence consubstantially embodied. If theology confined itself to rational, structural activities and excluded total perceptions of its data, the manifold images of the manifestation of the Word of God, the figures and parables of his Gospel, the mental and ritual symbols borrowed by the revelation of the mystery, the negative ways of approaching the divinity and the implications of the *praxis Ecclesiae,* it would be atrophied not only in its sources but also in its capacity for understanding and in the humanity of its witness.

This does not diminish in the slightest the requirements and advantages of the specific act of conceptualization. Some people fear it, either as a blow to the purity of the faith or as the procedure of an intellectual elite. In point of fact it is an operation proper to man, both when it is commanded by initial intuition and when it is perfected by silent contemplation. Admirable and delicate is the balance of theological "reason", whose "reasons" can never match the mystery. The work of the Council, including the painstaking elaboration of texts and words in the commissions, is a perfect example of this "reason" at work.

All the forms, all the equipment, all the levels of this reason will be deployed provided that epistemological values are respected and the modesty of the most inquisitive faith is spared. In days gone by, Abelard forgot to respect either this modesty or the Scholastic basis. Thus we range from the simple nominal definition, scarcely more than the biblical utterance, to the deduction of "conclusions"—a limited operation, it is true, and one not characteristic of theology. In these forms and at these levels, it is important to situate the argument of expedience, whose name gives some indication of the epistemological density of the faith and which is almost certainly the most appropriate both to the object of faith and to the discretion of the believer.

Of all the resources of this *cogitatio fidei,* let us single out the analogy of faith, which Vatican Council I regarded as an outstanding operation of the believer's understanding and which was constantly employed at Vatican Council II, with the resultant advantage that the most diverse texts, constitutions, decrees, declarations and messages display a rare homogeneity.

Finally, we should recognize the necessity and validity of theological *systems.* The Church's magisterium, especially in a council dominated by the notion of purity of witness, does not pronounce any judgment on this point apart from that on orthodoxy, even if sometimes it goes to the limit, as in this or that controversy over the eucharist. But the system—that is, the complete construction of the revealed fact into a totality based on selected principles—fulfills a requirement of the human mind. There could hardly be respect for an evangelism which declined to adopt a structure of this sort in a world where "ideologies" canalize the aspirations of men and the fate of whole peoples. The relativity of the choices made can very well correspond to their necessity. Pluralism does not harm the unity of the faith.

Let me end by underlining the urgency, for theology, of both epistemological and functional unity. The divisions introduced by modern theology gave a useful sanction to progress in analyses and methods: speculative-practical, positive-speculative, moral-casuistic, ascetic-mystical, scholastic-spiritual and, more recently, pastoral, missionary and so on. But these divisions soon collapsed under their own weight; their application needs to be controlled. It is indisputable that the theology of the Council is characterized by its unity as well as its value as a synthesis and as a reaction against the fragmentation of scholarly specialization, so much so that it will prove very difficult to classify the texts according to the categories of the manuals. In truth, the Word of God, like the life of the Spirit, tends toward unity, the sign of perfection, where knowledge and action are themselves united. Theological science is a kind of wisdom.

PART II
BIBLIOGRAPHICAL
SURVEY

Herbert Hammans/Mönchengladbach, W. Germany

Recent Catholic Views on the Development of Dogma

There has always been a development of dogma in the Church. It was not so much the fact of this development but rather its nature, its limits and the factors that contributed to it which were discussed by Catholic theologians in the 19th century. This was a result of the progress of the idea of development in philosophy and science and also a result of serious study of the history of dogma. Within the Church the philosophy of Anton Günther, modernism and the dogmatic definitions of the immaculate conception and bodily assumption of Mary demanded an explanation of this development.

The Catholic theologians of Tübingen, J. S. Drey, J. A. Möhler and J. E. Kuhn, tried to work out the Catholic idea of dogmatic development, and their influence is still active. John Henry Newman was forced through his personal experience to find a basic explanation for this phenomenon. The result was his great *Essay on the Development of Christian Doctrine* (1845). Scholastic theology of this century, which had to deal with the development of dogma for the above-mentioned reasons, moved in purely rational categories: development lies in making explicit what is already implicitly contained in a statement. On the whole, the dispute between Catholic theology and modernism remained really inadequate. However, there were some trends among several theologians that pointed to a more comprehensive explanation, and this holds particularly for M. Blondel [1] whose scrutiny of the idea of tradition will be more extensively examined below.

The more recent attempts to find a solution to this complex problem—attempts made since the heat of the modernist controversy abated toward the end of World War I—may be roughly divided into three groups: the historical approach, the intellectual (or rational) approach and the theological approach.

Those who approached the problem historically tried to find the explicit knowledge of the truths of faith in as early an age as possible, which, from their point of view, was a valid procedure. They assume that there was already in the apostolic age, in one way or another, an explicit knowledge of dogmas that were later defined. However, since these attempts led to historical impossibilities and started from the conviction that there was very little scope for a development of dogma, they were almost universally abandoned.[2]

During the 19th century Scholastic theologians tried to solve the problem by turning to the controversial issue of the dogmatic value of a theological conclusion—i.e., that the new dogmatic statement is derived from a revealed statement by means of a syllogism. This kind of discussion arose in the late Scholastic period in very different circumstances; however, it was now used for this particular issue and led them to see in a new dogma simply a logical conclusion, arrived at by ratiocination, and thus the equivalent of an originally revealed Christian reality. This

[1] This brief survey is based on H. Hammans, *Die neueren katholischen Erklärungen der Dogmenentwicklung.* Beiträge zur neueren Geschichte der katholischen Theologie, 7 (Essen, 1965). Details and arguments for somewhat bare sounding statements in this article may be found there. The American edition (The Newman Press, Westminster, Maryland), in process of publication, incorporates further literature. The most important recent work is the section on the historicity of the communication of revelation by K. Rahner and K. Lehmann in J. Feiner and M. Löhrer, *Mysterium Salutis. Grundrisz heilsgeschichtlicher Dogmatik* (Einsiedeln, 1965), pp. 727-87, which relies for its references on my work; this bulletin in turn owes much to their work.

[2] The impossibility of these assumptions has been demonstrated for the typical case of Mary's virginity in "Virginitas in partu," in *Schriften zur Theologie* IV (Einsiedeln, 1960), pp. 173-205.

intellectual approach to the problem was mainly represented by R. M. Schultes, F. Marin-Sola and M. Tuyaerts, whose works appeared almost at the same time.[3] They differ from each other as follows: Schultes maintained that only what is revealed in a formally implicit way can become matter for a dogmatic definition; Tuyaerts and Marin-Sola went further, maintaining that what is virtually revealed—i.e., derived through a proper syllogism with the help of a new idea—is also declared by God and can therefore be matter for dogmatic definition. For the subtle analyses of ideas which characterize both tendencies, I must refer the reader to the relevant theological textbooks. Both these theses, which found much support, were subjected to a thorough philosophical, theological and historical examination[4] and found to be no longer tenable inasmuch as they were too radical and unilateral.

Dissatisfaction with this kind of purely logical explanation of development of dogma, concern with the dogmatic definition of Mary's bodily assumption, a more profound understanding of Newman and the theologians of Tübingen, the various influences of modern philosophy, and, finally, the change that came over the Church and over theology—all these factors stimulated the

[3] R. M. Schultes, *Introductio in historiam dogmatum* (Paris, 1922); M. Tuyaerts, *L'Evolution du dogme* (Louvain, 1919); F. Marin-Sola, *L'Evolution homogène du Dogme catholique,* I and II (Fribourg, [2]1924) = *La evolución homogénea del dogma católico* (Valencia, 1923).

[4] The labor of an historical investigation, most valuable for the history of theology at large as well as for this question, was undertaken by J. Alfaro, "El progreso dogmatico en Suarez: Problemi di teologia contemporanea," in *Anal. Greg.* 68 (1954), pp. 95-122; A. Lang, "Die Gliederung und die Reichweite des Glaubens nach Thomas von Aquin und den Thomisten. Ein Beitrag zur Erklärung der scholastischen Begriffe fides, haeresis und conclusio theologica," in *Divus Thomas* 20 (1942), pp. 207-36, 335-46; 21 (1943), pp. 79-97; *idem,* "Die conclusio theologica in der Problemstellung der Spätscholastik," in *Divus Thomas* 22 (1944), pp. 256-90; *idem,* "Der Bedeutungswandel der Begriffe fides und haeresis und die dogmatische Wertung der Konzilsentscheidungen von Vienne und Trient," in *Münch. Theol. Zeitschr.* 4 (1953), pp. 133-46; E. Pozo, *Contribución a la historia des las soluciones al problema del progreso dogmático* (Granada, 1957); *idem, La teoría del progreso dogmático en los teólogos de la escuela de Salamanca.* Bibliotheca Theologica Hispana I, 1 (Madrid, 1959); *idem,* "La teoría del progreso dogmático en Luis de Molina, S.J.," in *Archivo Teologico Granadino* 24 (1961), pp. 5-32.

search for a more adequate synthesis of everything that played
a part in this development of dogma. These new attempts are
described as the theological category of efforts because they better illustrate the *theo*logical character of the development of
dogma which is an unrepeatable phenomenon. But, since the
great works of Schultes and Marin-Sola, no one has yet tried to
produce a comprehensive theory. In the argument about the
previous attempts, several points of view as well as new particular factors have come to the fore. Thus I can only present
a survey which deals with these particular elements rather loosely
linked together. We should not overlook here the fact that all
the elements of the Church's life of faith participate in this unfolding of the revelation because of their inherent vitality so that
it is impossible to reduce them all to a single principle. Finally,
we should constantly remember that a complete theory is only
possible when the development of dogma is finished, and for us
that means, in fact, never. Therefore, the history of dogma remains full of surprises. Like all history, it is unrepeatable; it cannot be pinned down to unchanging laws and thus cannot be
attacked by appealing to such laws.

I

THE REVELATION

Any theory about the development of dogma rests essentially
on the idea of revelation. Many theologians object that those
who uphold the intellectual approach assume too easily that the
truth of revelation is above all and always expressed in definite
statements. For them the starting point of development of dogma
is provided by a whole complex of formulated statements. But
revelation is first of all a happening, a self-communication of
God to the created mind. Karl Rahner, to whom I owe the most
basic ideas on this question,[5] emphasizes this point: "At its origin

[5] K. Rahner, "Zur Frage der Dogmenentwicklung," in *Schriften zur
Theologie* I (Einsiedeln, 1954), pp. 49-90; *idem,* "Ueberlegungen zur
Dogmenentwicklung," in *Schriften zur Theologie* IV (Einsiedeln, 1960),

revelation is not the communication of a number of propositions
. . . but an historical dialogue between God and man in which
something happens and in which the communication is related
to an event, to an action of God." This event is the self-communication of God which is final and cannot be surpassed.

If God did not reveal himself, there would be no reason for
him to speak at all, since he could give all that is outside himself
and about which he could speak via the real creation of such
finite communications. But if he reveals himself, then the re-
ceiver of the revelation needs the light of the grace of faith to
lift him to the supernatural level. If this were not the case, then
God's speech would fall under the sway of the subjective pre-
condition of the human mind; this would reduce it to an element
of self-understanding of a mere creature, and it would no longer
be a real self-revelation of God. Therefore, we have a specific
situation in the knowledge of revelation.

Within the sphere of natural knowledge there are two ways
of acquiring this knowledge: (1) a real experience of the reality
in itself or in its effects; (2) reliance on the witness of another.
Because, as believers, we have to rely on a verbal witness to the
revelation, people too easily conclude that we must think of
revelation in terms of this second kind of knowledge, and therefore in terms of a witness in the shape of mere words. But the
word of revelation which reaches us in grace implies a higher
medium: the word contains the reality itself. And this does not
only hold for the apostolic age when the revelation was effected,
but also for the post-apostolic age of the Church in which the
development of dogma takes place. "Spirit and word together
create the permanently active possibility of an experience which
is, in principle, the same as that of the apostles, even though our
experience is always essentially founded on that of the apostles,
since it rests on the transmitted word of the apostles, and,
founded on that, continues it." [6]

pp. 11-50; *idem,* "Dogmenentwicklung," in *Lex. Theol. u. Kirche* III
(Freiburg, ²1959), pp. 457-63; the quotation appears in "Zur Frage . . ."
p. 59.

[6] K. Rahner, "Zur Frage . . ." *loc. cit.,* p. 80.

This statement might imply the theological truth which per-
sisted in the Church until the Council of Trent—namely, that
revelation and inspiration continue in the Church. This older
view cannot be explained away as unsatisfactory terminology,
but rather must be seen as proof of a living awareness that revelation, fully understood, always contains an inner and an outer
element.[7] However much we stress the aspect of this inner reality
in revelation, it is obvious that we should not overlook or underrate its formulation in words.

However, revelation as an outward process does happen not
only in words but also in deeds. N. Sanders has pointed out that
the supernatural order brought about by Christ has assumed, in
himself and in the Church, visible forms which may give rise to
certain perceptions in the course of the Church's history.[8] H.
Rondet also sees revelation in Christ's deeds and in the whole
process of his life and his teaching—for example, in his attitude
toward his mother, through which he revealed to us the place of
Mary in the order of salvation.[9] In the same way, the *Dogmatic
Constitution on Divine Revelation* of Vatican Council II recognizes that "revelation is effected in interrelated actions and
words".[10]

How, then, should we think of the beginning of revelation in
the subject who receives it? On this point Newman's thought is
rich with suggestions. Christianity, according to him, came into

[7] Cf. K. Rahner and K. Lehmann, *Mysterium Salutis* I, *loc. cit.*, pp.
737-38; J. Ratzinger, "Offenbarung-Schrift-Ueberlieferung," in *Trierer
Theol. Zeitschr.* 67 (1938), pp. 13-27; *idem*, "Ein Versuch zur Frage
des Traditionsbegriffs," in K. Rahner and J. Ratzinger, *Offenbarung
und Ueberlieferung.* Quaestiones disputatae, 25 (Freiburg, 1965), pp.
25-69; Y. Congar, *Tradition and Traditions in the Church* (New York:
Macmillan, 1966), contains a rich collection of tests which prove that
revelation and inspiration continue in the Church.
[8] "Openbaring, Traditie, Dogma-ontwikkeling," in *Studia Catholica* 15
(1939), pp. 1-12, 111-29.
[9] H. Rondet, "La définibilité de l'Assomption," in *Etudes Mariales.*
Bulletin de la Société Française d'Etudes Mariales (Paris, 1948), pp.
59-95.
[10] *Dogmatic Constitution on Divine Revelation*, n. 2 (Glen Rock, N.J.:
Paulist Press, 1966), p. 58; also cf. nn. 4 and 7.

the world as an idea rather than as an institution. This idea contains a life. The impression which the mind receives from it in a first intuition is not yet a full understanding. It must develop in the mind and there unfold its various aspects which are not yet consciously perceived at the start. Thus there arises through human thought in its various ways, described by Newman with psychological finesse, a whole system of thoughts that nevertheless is not much more than the representation of a single idea.[11]

This idea of a global experience within the happening of the revelation, which precedes articulate formulae and which is an inexhaustible source for further articulation, can be found in several authors. Maurice Blondel had already pointed out that the Church's tradition does not only presuppose the texts; at the same time there is a constantly new experience which allows tradition in a sense to keep control of the texts instead of being subject to them.[12] Henri de Lubac holds that there was a wholly concrete and live comprehension at the beginning in which numerous formulae remained hidden, and this mysterious beginning may be called "the whole of dogma" (le tout du dogme).[13] He received much support from H. M. Köster, particularly as regards the teaching about Mary in the perception of which "a not straightaway formulated, yet quite definite overall impression played an important part".[14]

[11] These rather summary indications can easily be misunderstood, like so much in Newman's thought. For a better understanding of them I therefore refer to J. H. Walgrave, Newman. Le développement du dogme (Tournai, 1957), which explains his teaching on development in the light of his personality, philosophy, psychology and apologetics.

[12] Geschichte und Dogma. Mit Einführungen von J. B. Metz und R. Marle (Mainz, 1963), pp. 69-70; Les premiers écrits de M. Blondel (Paris, 1956), pp. 149-228.

[13] H. de Lubac, "Le problème du développement du dogme," in Rech. Sc. Rel. 35 (1948), pp. 130-60.

[14] H. Köster, Unus Mediator. Gedanken zur marianischen Frage (Limburg, 1950); idem, "Das theologische Gewissen und die marianische Frage. Beobachtungen und Bemerkungen," in Theol. u. Glaube 40 (1950), pp. 393-422; idem, "Grundfragen der theologischen Erkenntnislehre. Zur Kontroverse um das neue Dogma," in Theol. u. Glaube 42 (1952), pp. 248-62. The quotation occurs on p. 253 of "Grundfragen . . ."

Unfortunately these indications were only slightly developed in the philosophical and theological sense, and they were therefore sharply attacked. Consequently, Karl Rahner tried to expand them somewhat. In the natural sphere there is already a kind of knowledge, unformulated in definite sentences, that provides a starting point for a mental development, and this development then leads gradually to formulation in sentences. This never lacks a certain measure of reflective articulation; it is even better understood through this progressive reflection so that the originally inarticulate knowledge of something and the reflective articulate knowledge of it are mutually interdependent and progressive elements of a single experience. Such an original basic knowledge was already there in the apostles, received in this case, of course, from the historical revelation in Christ. "Christ as the living medium between God and the world . . . is the object of an experience which is more simple, more comprehensive, more modest and yet richer than the individual formulae through which one can exploit this experience in a basically unlimited progressive manner." [15] Therefore, even in the apostolic age there was room for theology, for development, for an advance from what was possessed in a spiritual but unreflective way to a more precise formulation. In short, there was already a development of dogma within the sacred writings, and Rahner sees this development as the model of all further development of dogma.[16] In principle there is also room for such a comprehensive experience in the post-apostolic age.

It seems to me that this thought can be most helpful toward a satisfactory explanation of development of dogma, even though it still requires further study with regard to its origin, its foundation and its more precise elaboration. It may also help to explain the plenitude of the apostolic age, to which tradition has always clung, without having to accept that the apostles possessed a

[15] K. Rahner, "Zur Frage der Dogmenentwicklung," *loc. cit.,* p. 78; *idem, Mysterium Salutis* I, *loc. cit.,* pp. 758-59.

[16] K. Rahner, "Ueberlegungen zur Dogmenentwicklung," *loc. cit.,* pp. 14-16; *idem,* "Theologie in Neuen Testament," in *Schriften zur Theologie* V (Einsiedeln, 1962), pp. 33-53.

fully articulate or at least immediately understandable knowledge of the whole content of revelation. There are many things of which they had no explicit knowledge; yet, in a sense, they knew all inasmuch as they embraced the whole reality of God's saving act and lived spiritually in this reality. And because they "knew" it in a fulfilled manner, the Church's awareness of the faith in a later age is not superior to the simple awareness of the apostles.

II

EXPRESSION AND WORD

However highly we may appreciate the spiritual force of the unarticulated "whole of dogma", dogmatic development nevertheless remains bound up with the earlier formulations of the faith. Since these formulations, in fact, were expressed in sentences, we have to ask ourselves what precisely these sentences contain, and in order to arrive at least at some rough assessment, we must consider to what extent these sentences are derived from God and to what extent from human beings.

The former question deals with the matter, so topical today, of the full meaning of scripture—what has been called the *sensus plenus*. In recent years J. Coppens has written extensively on this subject in various publications: "The full meaning is the biblical meaning in depth as God himself intended it in the revelation and inspiration of a divine word, usually beyond the consciousness of the sacred author as intended in the literal sense." [17] The sacred author could not know this full meaning because it was not given to him together with the literal meaning, but what he says is homogeneous with this full meaning. This full sense is derived from the literal sense through new revelations and in the light of the whole body of scripture and the influence which the text itself has exercised in the course of the development of faith.

[17] *Vom christlichen Verständnis des Alten Testamentes. Les harmonies des deux Testaments.* Bibliographical supplement and bibliography of J. Coppens. Folia Lovaniensia, 3-4 (Bruges, 1952), p. 21.

How this perception comes about is also something which several authors have tried to explain. E. Schillebeeckx refers to the light of faith;[18] A. Kolping speaks of a clear and acute insight given through grace to the Church, which then also perceives what can only be seen vaguely, unclearly, by a purely natural perception and cannot be apprehended in a natural manner.[19] Karl Rahner points out that a human speaker can never fully survey the result of what he says, but God can. He can intend the unfolding of his statements in these very statements beforehand. If, in this way, something is deduced from what he has said, God has not formally said it but he has nevertheless communicated it.[20] Similar ideas can be found in E. Dhanis who shows somewhat subtly that a truth signifies only indirectly but testifies formally and therefore can be clung to with divine faith.[21]

As a human word the word of revelation, especially the word of scripture, opens up large fields for this process of derivation. The biblical author says many things through the manner in which he writes and composes his message. His repetitions and his allusions to other texts reveal his intentions. Apart from this, he writes as a member of the Church and has his place in the theology of the Church of his age. Therefore, what he says may be interpreted in the light of the whole of scripture. The particular nature of the Semitic thought, which is open and dynamic and often means more than it says, prevents us from reducing scriptural statements to clearly confined premises.

This holds for the nature of human sentences in general. Every human sentence has a certain vagueness of contour; an

---

[18] E. Schillebeeckx, *Offenbarung und Theologie*. Gesammelte Schriften, I (Mainz, 1965), pp. 149-50.

[19] A. Kolping, "Zur theologischen Erkenntnismethode anläszlich der Definition der leiblichen Aufnahme Mariens in den Himmel," in *Divus Thomas* 65 (1951), pp. 81-105.

[20] K. Rahner, "Zur Frage . . ." *loc. cit.*, pp. 70-75.

[21] E. Dhanis wrote on explicit and implicit revelation in "Lo sviluppo del dogma secondo la Dottrina Cattolica," in *Relazioni lette nella seconda settimana teologica* of Sept. 24-28, 1951 (Rome, 1953), pp. 168-218, esp. pp. 175-207.

explanation cannot express all that is implied in thought and word. However, it can be understood in the same way by the hearer, who can then express it more explicitly in sentences, perhaps in the shape of a deduction, without thereby going beyond the field covered by what the speaker has formally communicated in the first place. Such an unfolding is not limited to the individual sentence, but can take from a series of statements what served as background and basic assumption in individual statements. This is the way in which biblical theology goes about its task.[22]

Here B. Welte's contribution to the discussion is helpful.[23] Revelation must reach the man to whom it is addressed through intelligent listening. Such an understanding cannot be limited to the material complexity of the word to be understood. It must penetrate deeper until it reaches an understanding of the one living and all-animating principle of life, the origin of the whole complex reality of the word. When it touches this principle, it can from that vantage point understand everything else and progressively come to statements which derive effortlessly from the Spirit of the revelation. It can then show itself as contained in the words and utterances in which the Spirit of the revelation expressed himself, without these words being capable of showing the full content in its manifold separate aspects.

Going beyond these considerations Karl Rahner thinks that the objective implication of a statement in different sentences— which is what we have been talking about up till now—is not enough to allow us to say that these sentences or statements were always believed by the Church. It is possible that some known statements imply something objective; nevertheless, this something may simply lie beyond this knowledge of these sentences and therefore cannot be said to be held in faith. Therefore, it demands, beyond an objective implication, a subjective

[22] K. Rahner, "Zur Frage . . ." *loc. cit.,* pp. 81-86.
[23] B. Welte, *Philosophische Bemerkungen zum Begriff der Offenbarung.* Paper read at the meeting of a theological working group in Oct. 1957 at Innsbruck. For the notion of understanding, cf. K. Lehmann, "Verstehen," in *Lex. Theol. u. Kirche* X (Freiburg, ²1965), pp. 737-38.

one which makes it possible to say of a truth that it has always been known by the Church and the faithful, even though it was not grasped in an explicit and reflective manner.[24]

III

LOGIC AND ITS CERTAINTY

For those who explained the development of dogma on purely intellectual lines, it was the syllogism, constructed according to the rules of logic, which determined the way and the measure of the kind of thinking that led to new theological and dogmatic perceptions. There are many objections to this narrowing down of development, which is rooted in a limitation of theology to a theology based on logical conclusions.[25] The upholders of this approach begin by asking whether a truth is definable or not. They do not ask how the conviction of this definability of a truth arose in the Church. Therefore, they see only the result and not the way that led to the result. But the way that leads to the discovery of a truth is not that of a deduction by way of syllogisms. Even in ordinary life the result must have become clear along very different ways before we can look for the logical premises at all. Schillebeeckx points out that these thinkers confuse the logical aspect of thought with the psychological aspect. Psychologically, thinking is nothing less than the total perception of experience which is dominated by the object. The syllogism only controls its noetic structure. The conclusions were already present in an unnoticed way in the consciousness where they were discovered through the perception of experience and through reflective analysis.[26] There is a difference between the

[24] "Dogmenentwicklung," *loc. cit.*, p. 459; *Mysterium Salutis* I, *loc. cit.*, p. 759; for the concept of subjective implication, cf. A. Röper, *Die anonymen Christen* (Mainz, 1963), pp. 24-38.

[25] For some observations, cf. H. Hammans, *op. cit.* (footnote 1), pp. 167-69; E. Schillebeeckx, *Offenbarung und Theologie*, pp. 89-91, 109-30.

[26] E. Schillebeeckx, *op. cit.*, pp. 62-63, 114-15.

logic of discovery and that of checking up on it.[27] Perception takes shape through a thousand observations that have only been grasped instinctively, and they can only with difficulty be fitted into a chain of syllogistic formulae, if at all.

Moreover, such theologians forget too easily that statements of the faith are concerned with mysteries of salvation which cannot be seized by merely human logic. Dogma bursts our notions wide open.[28] In any case the discussion is often permeated with irrational undertones which destroy the value of human concepts in theology altogether. They are damned in the discussion by their very limitation.

One can certainly say that the rise of a conviction of faith in the Church cannot be explained by logical deduction. Nor is the first discovery of such a conviction prompted by the written deposit of the revelation but rather by the manner in which the truths on which a new dogma is based have been proclaimed and fulfilled in the Church.

This does not exclude the fact that there is a logical connection between later formulated dogmas and the statements of the original revelation, but this should in any case not be understood merely as a connection between the explicit and its formally or virtually implicit contents. This purely syllogistic approach has been disproved by recent historical and systematic research.[29] The idiom of scripture mentioned above, the peculiar nature of theology which has to use the science of history rather than that of mathematics in the study of its sources, the nature of intellectual sciences in general where one rarely meets with a clear and final argument and where one reaches the object rather through successive approaches—all this should make it clear that, in the unfolding of dogma, theology should incorporate the same factors that play a part in all human thought within a human action. One can observe a certain continuity in the history of dogma. The connection between the old and the

---

[27] H. Rondet, op. cit., p. 67.
[28] H. de Lubac, op. cit., p. 148.
[29] K. Rahner and K. Lehmann, Mysterium Salutis I, loc. cit., p. 760.

new is "not something that is completely outside history but that also lies at least in the historical transmission of the original message and is therefore from beginning to end a fact which can be historically perceived".[30]

Of course, theological reflection does not necessarily lead to certainty, even if by certainty one does not understand the metaphysical certainty of an inclusive syllogism in the sense of Marin-Sola. How, then, does such certainty come about? According to many theologians, it suffices that there be a general consensus of the faith among the faithful when it is at least recognized as the consensus of the Church by the sense of faith of the pope.[31] P. Rousselot, who pursues an idea of Newman's, and Karl Rahner point to a conviction which rests on motives that are real but cannot be explained in such a way that everyone can understand them. This conviction can afterward be developed without completely reaching the trustworthiness of that overall certainty which already existed. What individual theologians have to offer is, as it were, a contribution offered to the understanding of the faith of the whole Church and the magisterium. Only the awareness of the faith of the Church as a whole can decide whether a theological contribution is acceptable. It also often happens that after a decision by the magisterium the evidence of the reasons becomes clearer because the decision as such has its own inner evidence.[32]

E. Dhanis, who cannot accept this kind of argument, tries to solve the question with the help of the Thomistic theology of the light of faith. Faith is not possible without an inner, dark invitation by the Father. This invitation concerns the revelation proclaimed by the Church. But it can also be extended to derivations from it which are only probable in character. The con-

---

[30] K. Rahner, "Ueberlegungen . . ." loc. cit., p. 12.

[31] Cf., for instance, M. D. Koster, Volk Gottes im Wachstum des Glaubens (Heidelberg, 1950), p. 128.

[32] P. Rousselot, "Note sur le développement du dogme," in Rech. Sc. Rel. 37 (1950), pp. 113-20; idem, Die Augen des Glaubens (Christ heute V, 2), with an introduction by J. Trütsch (Einsiedeln, 1963), pp. 68-69 = Les yeux de la foi); K. Rahner, "Ueberlegungen . . ." loc. cit., pp. 31-36, 45.

jecture of an individual that a given truth might be revealed becomes a certainty through the growing convergence of such con-
jectures within the Church and can then serve the magisterium
as a help for its decision.[33] Similar suggestions have been made
by C. Dillenschneider and E. Schillebeeckx.[34]

IV

TRADITION

The intellectual approach sees in tradition first of all a source
which contains revelation alongside of scripture so that one can
derive dogmas from it. This well-known but really too static concept of tradition cannot do justice to the fullness of that phenomenon or to the intricate interconnection of either scripture
and tradition or tradition and the Church. And so since the 19th
century there has developed in theology a tendency to see in
the post-biblical tradition not so much a static quantity, but
rather a dynamic and vital process (active tradition) that reflects upon and explains the divine revelation which found its
first expression, guaranteed by God, in scripture (objective tradition) with the participation of all the members of the Church
(subjective tradition).[35] As such it becomes more of a "declar-
ing" tradition than a constitutive one, and as such is interesting
for an explanation of dogmatic developments.

The ideas of the school of Tübingen, particularly those of
J. A. Möhler, were popular because for them the tradition in
the subjective sense is "the specific sense of the Church which is
already present in the Church and propagates itself there but
which nevertheless cannot be thought of without its content".[36]

[33] E. Dhanis, op. cit., pp. 207-17.
[34] C. Dillenschneider, Le sens de la foi et le progrès dogmatique du
mystère marial (Rome, 1954), pp. 81-105; E. Schillebeeckx, op. cit., pp.
67-74.
[35] The Dogmatic Constitution on Divine Revelation of Vatican Council
II also states that the sacred writings are more profoundly understood
through tradition (n. 8). However, it offers no decision on the nature of
tradition.
[36] Symbolik oder Darstellung der dogmatischen Gegensätze der Kath-

Newman also held, independently of Möhler, that the notion of implicit thought made it possible for the post-apostolic Church to arrive at a living and concrete interpretation of the sources through which the revelation reaches us. But it was particularly Blondel who broke through a too narrow notion of tradition. According to him, tradition does not transmit a series of venerable sentences or actions from the past but rather the living reality itself. It rests on the texts, but at the same time on an experience which is happening all the time and which allows it to dominate the texts. It formulates truths which have been lived in the past without being able to express them. "Even when it discovers something it still has the feeling of only having rediscovered it faithfully." In this way it passes from "what is lived implicitly to what is known explicitly".[37] Tradition is then identical with "action"—obviously understood as the "action" of his philosophy.

These thoughts, for which Blondel found little understanding among his contemporaries,[38] are today exercising a strong influence on modern theology. This can be seen from these words of A. Liégé, chosen from many others: "The real theory of development is the living and active tradition; it is Pentecost continued." [39] M.-D. Chenu, Y. Congar, C. Dillenschneider, R. Draguet, J. R. Geiselmann, H. de Lubac, Hugo Rahner, Karl Rahner and E. Schillebeeckx think along the same lines.[40] In view of this trend, the theology that used to identify the magisterium with tradition has declined.

V

THE SENSE OF FAITH

The facts of the history of dogma which show that the ordinary faithful with their piety also take part in the unfolding of the

---

oliken und Protestanten nach ihren öffentlichen Bekentnisschriften, ed. by J. R. Geiselmann (Darmstadt, 1958), p. 415.
    [37] M. Blondel, op. cit., pp. 69-70.
    [38] Cf., for example, J. Bainvel, A. d'Alès, L. de Grandmaison, and many ideas of A. Gardeil; also cf. H. Hammans, op. cit., pp. 90-97.
    [39] "Dogme," in Catholicisme III (Paris, 1952), pp. 951-62, esp. p. 961.
    [40] H. Hammans. op. cit., pp. 261-62.

truths of faith, the difficulty of making later dogmas derive from an originally revealed statement through the application of creaking methods, the now flourishing theology of the Church and of the laity—all these factors have paved the way for a perception of what is revealed, which is usually called the sense of faith. The consensus of the faithful has always been recognized as of major dogmatic importance in Catholic theology. Their witness is a means toward perceiving what is revealed. Newman, above all, attributed great value to the witness of the laity in questions of faith.[41] However, we must distinguish this consensus of the faith which can be established from that other sense of faith which is a kind of spontaneous force which judges in matters of faith. For Newman it is nothing else than the illative sense, the sense of inference of the whole Church.[42] It was first introduced into the Scholastic theories about the development of dogma by Marin-Sola; the magisterium also is aware of its force.[43]

It is obvious that the sense of faith is influenced by the light of faith and the gifts of the Spirit. It is less clear what serves as the natural substratum for its operation. M. D. Koster, who indeed has a very great respect for the sense of faith, sees there "the receptivity and adaptability of the spirit, linked with desire and inclination, as it touches the individual in what belongs to him and is proper to him".[44] However, his interpretation is poorly based since he makes his sources say more than they con-

---

[41] For the witness of the laity in matters of faith, see his *On Consulting the Faithful in Matters of Faith.*

[42] H. Fries, "J. H. Newmans Beitrag zum Verständnis der Tradition," in *Die mündliche Ueberlieferung. Beiträge zum Begriff der Tradition,* ed. by M. Schmaus (Munich, 1957), pp. 63-122, esp. p. 119.

[43] J. Filograssi, *De sanctissima Eucharistia.* Quaestiones dogmaticae selectae (Rome, ⁶1957), pp. 44-45; Pius XII, Encyclical Letter *Ad caeli reginam* (Nov. 18, 1954), in which he founded the introduction of the feast of Mary as Queen among other things on the "religious sense with which the Christian people are imbued": *A.A.S.* 46 (1954), pp. 625-40, esp. p. 638; cf. also the *Dogmatic Constitution on Divine Revelation, op. cit.,* n. 5; *Dogmatic Constitution on the Church,* nn. 12 and 35 (Glen Rock, N.J.: Paulist Press, 1965).

[44] M. D. Koster, *op. cit.,* p. 62; *idem, Die Firmung im Glaubenssinn der Kirche* (Münster, 1948); *idem,* "Theologie, Theologien und Glaubenssinn," in *Theol. u. Seelsorge* (Paderborn, 1943), pp. 82-90.

tain. C. Balić appeals to principles that are applied in a hidden—
one might say, instinctive—activity; J. Filograssi has recourse
to judgments of sympathy which spring from an habitual knowledge; C. Dillenschneider, who has produced the most thorough
study on this question, relies on an experiential contact with the
object of faith, a contact added by God to the power of spontaneous perception.[45] M. Seckler brings it back to "a perception rooted in the dynamism of the mind, a perception of an
unreflective kind, which uses logic without abandoning itself to
it because the object of the perception of faith is at the same
time the principle of this perception".[46] To this should be added
the above-mentioned interpretations about the logic of discovery
with reference to Rahner, Rondet and Rousselot.

All the theologians who have dealt with the sense of faith have
warned against overrating it. The consensus of faith which
springs from it is difficult to define. The faith of a large part of
the people is weak, inclined to be one-sided, and is useless for
more subtle questions. It is the function of the magisterium to
judge it, and this magisterium stimulates it, watches over it, but
is also bound to take note of it.

VI

The Perception of Revealed Truth as Dogma

Dogmatic development causes the Church to recognize in a
reflective manner a truth as revealed by God. How does this
truth pass into the Church's reflective consciousness? Karl
Rahner was the first to draw attention to this key problem of
development of dogma.[47] This question cannot be answered by
appealing to an ecclesiastical definition or to the conclusiveness

---

[45] C. Balić, "Il senso cristiano e il progresso del dogma," in *Lo sviluppo
del dogma, loc. cit.,* pp. 106-34; J. Filograssi, *op. cit.,* pp. 41-47; C. Dillenschneider, *op. cit.,* pp. 317-27.

[46] "Glaubenssinn," in *Lex. Theol. u. Kirche* IV (Freiburg, ²1960), pp.
945-48, esp. p. 947.

[47] K. Rahner, "Ueberlegungen . . ." *loc. cit.,* pp. 40-49; *idem, Mysterium Salutis I, loc. cit.,* pp. 774-76.

of the arguments we have discussed inasmuch as they can offer no certainty of faith, or to the fundamental right of the Church to define something. The knowledge of this right is no basis for that further element of consent which belongs to faith. A similar problem exists in the case of any free decision which is preceded by an insight, but which, in spite of this, has no more than its own evidence once the decision is taken.

Rahner notes that a similar question arises when we pass from the *preambula fidei* (the preliminary approach to faith), on a qualitatively lower level, to faith itself, although in the present discussion it refers to the faith of the whole Church, the faith which the Church represents reflectively (explicitly) as it progresses. Moreover, it starts here from a revelation already believed in, and not from a state of non-belief. Therefore, this argument allows him in this discussion about the transition to bring in a discussion about the "analysis of faith". Suggestions in this direction may be found in Newman, who appeals to the illative sense for an explanation of the perception of both the credibility of the revelation and the revealed character of an individual truth; they may also be found in Rousselot's treatment of the "eyes of faith" and in Dhanis, Rondet and Schillebeeckx.

VII

THE MAGISTERIUM

When the Church's magisterium proposes it as such, a revealed truth becomes dogma. Even in the way it comes about, the development of dogma depends on the magisterium, because those factors which lie outside the magisterium, whether they come from this magisterium itself or are directed toward it, belong to the community's thinking about the faith which is led by this magisterium.

Since such an ecclesiastical decision implies that the development which led to it was justified, it was tempting to justify every dogmatic development by simply referring to the justification of the magisterium as such on the lines of fundamental theology. This was the line taken by Draguet, at least for the case where no historical or rational proof is available.[48] L. Charlier and R. Spaemann, starting from various points, maintain that our theological notions are unable to arrive at a clear advance in theological perception since only the magisterium can formulate the necessary statements under the guidance of the Spirit.[49] Dillenschneider credits the magisterium with a special charisma for penetrating and distinguishing the truth when a rational deduction does not lead to certainty.[50] The same considerations led to the assertion that—in principle and not only in fact—a theologian can perceive a truth as coming from revelation only in the light of the magisterium, or that, when theologians have established that there is a gap in our perception, it can be filled through the assistance of the Spirit in the Church's definition.[51]

This theological agnosticism is firmly rejected by Y. Congar and Karl Rahner. They point out that the magisterium, materially speaking, must rely on what is proposed by the Church, but that, after a definition is given, theology still has the task to justify it, even when the Church in its decisions appeals to its authority and not to rational deductions. To reduce the theology of the development of dogma to a teaching about the magisterium would reduce the faith to a set of individual propositions which would find their only coherence in the authority of the magisterium. Faith would then be identical with obedience.[52]

[48] "L'évolution des dogmes," in *Apologétique. Nos raisons de croire. Réponse aux objections*, ed. by M. Brillant and M. Nédoncelle (Paris, ²1948), pp. 1097-1122, esp. p. 1121. Without excluding other arguments, Y. Congar agrees with him in *La Foi et la Théologie* (Tournai, 1962), pp. 117-18.
[49] L. Charlier, *Essai sur le problème théologique* (Thuilles, 1938), pp. 64, 140-41; R. Spaemann, "Das neue Dogma und die Dogmentheorie," in *Münch. Theol. Zeitschr.* 3 (1952), pp. 151-60, esp. pp. 158-59.
[50] C. Dillenschneider, *op. cit.*, pp. 80-81, 360.
[51] B. Altaner, "Zur Frage der Definierbarkeit der Assumptio BMV," in *Theol. Rev.* 46 (1950), pp. 5-20, esp. p. 18.
[52] K. Rahner, "Ueberlegungen . . ." *loc. cit.*, pp. 25-29; *idem, Mysterium Salutis* I, *loc. cit.*, pp. 769-70; Y. Congar, *Jalons pour une théologie du laicat* (English ed.: *Lay People in the Church* [Newman, 1965]).

VIII

Spirit and Grace

All theological discussion about the development of dogma is in agreement about the fact that the unfolding of the dogma is moved by the Spirit. All these explanations try to show that the Spirit is not confined to negative functions, as if the Spirit is merely there to preserve the magisterium in its definitions or the development in its actual process from error. They try to see his activity in a more positive light. Thus these theologians speak of an enlightening of the mind and an inspiration of the will, of the Spirit's control even of events in secular history through his supernatural providence, so that "every fact of civilization can be the starting point of a development of teaching in the Church".[53] In order to perceive the divine logic which links the original revelation with the developed faith, Dillenschneider requires a sense of faith and a special charisma of discernment; in the same way, those who accept the theory of the "full meaning" (*sensus plenus*) hold that the Church is endowed with a special grace of clear-sightedness and penetration.[54]

O. Semmelroth stresses the activity of the Spirit, particularly in the unfolding of dogmatic teaching.[55] He compares the word of revelation with the God-Man himself. Just as in him there is a human body, a human soul and, hidden in that, the divine Logos, so the word of revelation has a "word-body", a "word-meaning" and, hidden in that, a third divine principle which can only be perceived through the guiding activity of the Spirit,

---

[53] F. Cavallera, "A propos de la vie du dogme," in *Bull. Litt. Eccl.* 43 (1942), p. 69.

[54] C. Dillenschneider, *op. cit.*, pp. 80-81, 103, 360; A. Kolping, *op. cit.*, p. 90.

[55] "Antwort auf Frage und Einwurf," in *Das neue Dogma im Widerstreit. Ein Beitrag zum ökumenischen Gespräch*, ed. by O. Semmelroth (Würzburg, 1951), pp. 23-44; *idem*, "Wesen und Werden des Dogmas," in *Bindung und Freiheit des katholischen Denkens*. Probleme der Gegenwart um Urteil der Kirche, ed. by A. Hartmann (Frankfurt, 1952), pp. 216-33; *idem*, "Zeitalter des Hl. Geistes," in *Geist u. Leben* 32 (1959), pp. 166-79, esp. pp. 169-73.

just as is the case with the perception of the presence of the Logos in the God-Man.

Habitual factors such as the strength of faith and the light of faith also influence the development of dogma indistinguishably. As has already been mentioned, Dhanis appeals to the light of faith in order to explain how truths that can only be deduced from revelation with probability can nevertheless be accepted as having come from God in all certainty.[56] Schillebeeckx maintains that a strictly supernatural starting point is required because this is a matter of a development of faith.[57] He sees this starting point in the light of faith which stimulates us to believe in the outward revelation of the word.

Various factors contribute to this unfolding. The light of faith guarantees the revealed character of a truth thus developed. However, it cannot be recognized by the individual since it is buried in the human consciousness. But in the community of the Church, where dogmatic development comes about through participation of all the members, the light of faith steers toward a convergence of all, so that within the Church there grows the conviction that a statement actually makes something explicit that the Church has already accepted in practice for a long time and corresponds to the content of Christ's revelation. The theological argument, which is then discovered, is like the lucky word with which somebody expresses our most inner conviction for us. The magisterium has always paid attention to this development and judges the collective reaction of the believing community as brought about by the light of faith. This allows it to declare the result as dogma. It is, together with the light of faith of the whole community, the one structural principle of the unchangeability of the faith.

I have already mentioned Rahner's teaching of the self-communication of God to the spirit in his own reality. It opens up a new possibility for dogma to develop into a constantly wider unfolding of statements. It also leads to an increasing concentra-

---

[56] E. Dhanis, *op. cit.*, pp. 207-17.

[57] E. Schillebeeckx, *Offenbarung und Theologie*, pp. 67-74, 143-44, 152-53.

tion on the *a priority* of that unity which is the mystery of the Trinity itself. It seems to him that too few theologians think through to this unity as a task for theology.[58]

Therefore, the development of dogma completes that circular movement common to all creation, starting from God and involving all the forces of his creation, in order to adore his inexhaustible mystery for all eternity.

[58] "Ueberlegungen . . ." *loc. cit.,* pp. 36-40.

George A. Lindbeck/*New Haven, Conn.*

The Problem of
Doctrinal Development and
Contemporary Protestant Theology

There is little in contemporary Protestant discussions corresponding directly to the treatments of doctrinal development which have proliferated in Roman Catholic circles since the days of Newman and Moehler. Many of the same problems are dealt with extensively under the rubrics of scripture and tradition[1] or creeds and confessions,[2] but the fact that the Church's teachings in some sense develop beyond their scriptural starting point in the course of time is not itself a major theological problem for Protestants.

It is not a major problem because doctrinal development is not thought of as occurring in the strong sense in which it does for Roman Catholics—i.e., it does not result in infallible dogmatic definitions. Only scripture has this exalted a status within the Reformation tradition, and even here, so most contemporary writers say, it is not the words or the details which are without error, but rather the revelation to which the inspired authors testify in their very human ways.

Consequently, it is not the problem of development since the New Testament which preoccupies Protestant theologians, but

[1] Cf., for example, K. Skydsgaard and L. Vischer (eds.), *Schrift u. Tradition* (Zürich, 1963). Cf. especially the bibliography for the years 1930-1962, pp. 157-69.

[2] Cf., for example, G. Gloege, "Bekenntnis-dogmatisch," in *RGG* I, pp. 994ff.

rather the problem of development and variety within the New Testament period itself. In other words, hermeneutical questions of the unity of scripture and of demythologizing hold the center of attention.[3] They seem to threaten the traditional Protestant appeal to the canonical scriptures, taken as a whole, as the sole final arbiter of the Church's teachings. In comparison, difficulties arising from later developments are relatively insignificant.

Yet they are not unimportant, and they do raise theological problems. Their importance is reflected in the attitude of the Reformers toward creeds and confessions which they clearly thought of as indispensable to the proper ordering of the Church. They are needed as helpful, though insufficient, guides to sound preaching, teaching and practice, as defenses against anti-Christian forces, and as signs and instruments of the visible unity of the Church.[4] In our day, with the diminution of the various types of individualism fostered by the Enlightenment, pietism, revivalism and liberalism, such attitudes have once again become widespread. Among the Protestant writers who deal expressly with this issue, there are few who would not agree that every community develops authoritative teachings—either formally explicated or implicitly held—that express, defend and promote the consensus by which it lives, and that to the degree that the community is large, variegated and enduring, these teachings need to become explicit and official rather than remain implicit and informal. This is not merely a sociological and historical necessity. Faithfulness to the Gospel requires that the community of believers authoritatively confess the faith in new ways under new situations as was done at Barmen (1934) by a portion of the Church under nazism or as various American denominations have recently done in condemning racial segregation.

However, the Protestant has difficulties explaining the authority of these post-biblical developments because for him the au-

[3] J. Robinson and J. Cobb, The New Hermeneutic. New Frontiers in Theology, 2 (New York, 1964).

[4] E. Kinder, Glaube u. Kirche (Berlin, 1958), pp. 115-44; V. Vajta and H. Weissgerber (eds.), The Church and the Confessions (Philadelphia, 1963), pp. 162-88.

thority of the bible is unrestricted and unqualified. It would seem, therefore, that any development may be freely challenged by anyone at anytime in the name of the scriptural principle, and that this so relativizes and conditions all doctrinal, as well as liturgical and ecclesiastical, structures that they lose their effectiveness. The problem, in short, is to maintain the *sola scriptura* while still finding a place for development.

It will later be argued that this is by no means as difficult as one might think. Theologically, Protestants consider their problem of development less grave than the Catholic one. It is rather on the practical plane that difficulties arise, for the magisterial functions in the Protestant Churches have atrophied to such an extent that they find it very difficult to engage in constructive doctrinal development. The corporately effective doctrinal decisions, such as those taken at Vatican Council II, which are necessary for renewal, are beyond their present capacities. But most Protestants would claim that this *de facto* weakness of ecclesiastical structures is not a theologically necessary outcome of the basic Reformation position (any more than the medieval Great Schism was the incorrigible outcome of Catholic doctrine).

It is evident from what has already been said that the Protestant problematic is the reverse of the Catholic one. The Catholic starts with highly authoritative developments going far beyond what is explicitly in the bible, and must then explain how this is reconcilable with the primacy of scripture (to which he also is committed in view of the principle that scripture alone is inspired). The Protestant, beginning with the *sola scriptura,* needs to interpret the *sola* in such a way as not to exclude the development of doctrinal traditions possessing some degree of effective authority.[5]

In order to understand the way Protestants approach this problem, we should remind ourselves, first of all, of their basic

[5] In other words, *sola scriptura* is not used in opposition to tradition, but rather asserts that scripture is the sole reliable record of that early tradition which is the *norma normans non normata* in reference to all later traditions.

reasons for insisting on the *sola scriptura,* and, secondly, of why the 16th-century explanation of the relation of Church doctrine to scripture is no longer tenable.

The Protestant maintains that the *sola scriptura* helps preserve the lordship of Jesus Christ over his Church because it makes unmistakably clear that the public revelation, culminating and summed up in him, has been closed—i.e., is final. Every effort must be made to subject all later developments to the authority of the first historically determinate[6] witness to the historical revelation. Otherwise the ever-threatening danger will be increased that—in practice, even if not in theory—these later developments will come to rival or replace scripture. Thus in effect, even if this is not acknowledged, they will function as additions to the public revelation and as limitations on the sovereignty of the historically incarnate Lord.[7]

The way in which the Reformers reconciled the authority of creeds and confessions with the *sola scriptura* was by minimizing (as did everyone before modern times) the fact that they were developments. They were represented simply as summaries or compendiums of the teachings of the bible,[8] which was therefore viewed as the "sole source", and not simply the "sole norm", of doctrine. This approach assumed the "clarity of the bible": that is, it assumed that it could be shown by rational means—at least to the extent of confounding, if not persuading, the adversaries— that the bible contains a certain consistent "system" of doctrine. In other words, what was proposed was *scriptura sui ipsius interpres* (scripture is its own interpreter), in the sense that its

---

[6] Even if there is an apostolic oral tradition, it is not "historically determinate"—i.e., there is no objectively controllable way of separating it from later additions except to the degree that it has been written down, and consequently it cannot have a normative value equal to the apostolic tradition which has been written, namely, scripture. This is in agreement with Catholic authors such as K. Rahner, "Was ist eine dogmatische Aussage?" in *Schriften* V, pp. 78-79.

[7] Many Protestant authors agree that this is the crucial issue in the *sola scriptura.* Cf., for example, the essays by G. Ebeling and K. Skydsgaard in *Schrift u. Tradition* (footnote 1 *supra*); K. Barth, *Kirchliche Dogmatik* I, 2 (Zürich, 1932ff.), p. 641.

[8] Cf., for example, *Formula of Concord SD,* par. 1.

literal and historical sense provides internal evidence as to its hermeneutical center—i.e., as to the "clearer" parts in terms of which the more "obscure" should be interpreted.[9] For Luther, and in varying degrees for the other Reformers, this center was Jesus Christ himself, understood in terms of what, in the 16th century at any rate, seemed to be the only possible literal reading of the Pauline doctrine of justification. This enabled them to adopt Luther's words, *"Urgemus Christum contra scripturam"*,[10] and thereby reinterpret works such as the epistle of St. James which did not at first reading appear reconcilable with the Reformation's understanding of St. Paul.

The result was that the Reformers were able to develop and embody in the major Reformation confessions remarkably consistent and comprehensive interpretations of the total biblical witness. While such interpretations did not resolve all differences (e.g., between the Lutherans and the Calvinists), they were sufficiently similar so that the basic Reformation positions could be plausibly presented in terms of the canons of "objective exegesis". These canons were prevalent in those days as a kind of reproduction in capsule form of the main teachings of scripture over against the spiritualizing individualism of the sectarians on the left and the Catholic appeal to tradition on the right.

The principle that "scripture is its own interpreter" has not been surrendered by Protestant theologians.[11] However, the 16th-

[9] For a good summary of these points, cf. W. Pannenberg, "Was ist eine dogmatische Aussage?" in *Pro Veritate,* edited by E. Schlink and H. Volk (Münster, 1963), pp. 343-46.

[10] *Weimar Ausgabe* 39/I, p. 47; 40/I, pp. 458f.

[11] This is particularly evident in the fact that even extreme theological existentialists and "Christian secularists" usually argue for their positions, not primarily because of their presumed greater intelligibility or relevance to modern man, but on the grounds that the fundamental thrust of the biblical witness, as this is discovered by critical-historical exegesis, is opposed to "religion" and to all forms of "objectivizing belief". This is what distinguishes contemporary radical attacks on the doctrinal tradition of the Church from the often more rationalistic ones of the old liberalism. Cf. H. Braun, "Die Überwindung des Liberalismus auf der Ebene des Kritizismus," in *Verkündigung u. Forschung* (1951), fascicle 1/2. Also cf. C. Braaten and R. Harrisville (eds.), *Kerygma and History* (Nashville, 1962), pp. 9-54.

century view of the relation of scripture to creeds and confessions has become untenable as the result of advances in historical studies and awareness. The Church's doctrines are developments which "go beyond" scripture. Included in them are what appear to be novel elements in terms of objective historiography; clearly they are not simply distillations of biblical teaching. Consequently their status has become questionable because they can no longer be thought of as directly and immediately derived from scripture.

As we have already indicated, the problem of development, phrased in this particular way, is not widely discussed. Nevertheless, it is possible to identify a widespread—though largely implicit—Protestant consensus that doctrinal development is to be understood simply in terms of what I shall call "historical situationalism". The implications of this can be stated in six points.

1. Organismic analogies are sharply rejected.[12] Doctrinal development is not a matter of continuous and cumulative growth or explicitation of the Church's knowledge of revelation or—even worse from the Protestant's point of view—of the Church's self-awareness or self-understanding. The deposit of faith does not live in the consciousness of the Church in a partially germinal form and then gradually unfold into a more completely articulated body of truths. Formulations of a somewhat similar kind were once widespread in Protestant circles,[13] but with the passing of immanentistic, progressive, romantic liberalism they have virtually disappeared among theologians.

2. Turning now to the positive characterization of development, this tends to be viewed simply as a function of the differences in the situations in which the Church exists. It is possible to think in these situationalist terms because the Church's doctrines are thought of as the products of the dialogue in history

[12] E. Wolf, "Kerygma und Dogma," in *Antwort—K. Barth Festschrift* (Zürich, 1956), pp. 805f.
[13] W. Maurer, "Das Prinzip des Organischen in der evangelischen Kirchengeschichtsschreibung des 19," in *Jahrhunderts, Kerygma u. Dogma* 8 (1962), pp. 265-92. For F. C. Bauer, cf. P. Hodgson, *The Formation of Historical Theology* (New York, 1966), pp. 243ff.

between God and his people and as the historically conditioned and relative responses, interpretations and testimonies to the Word addressing man through the scriptural witness. Circumstances change radically, and so also do the problems and the questions for which Christians seek answers. The answers as such are not found in the bible which, as a thoroughly historical book, does not explicitly formulate answers to questions of which its authors were unaware. Therefore, the Church, in reliance upon the Holy Spirit and in attentive listening to God speaking through scripture, finds itself called upon to formulate new doctrinal answers to new questions.

3. There is general agreement that developments, far from being regrettable because they go beyond the bible, are necessary to the essential continuity, vitality and renewal of the Church. This is not only because they are needed for the sake of relevance and intelligibility, but also because they are required in order to maintain old truths. Traditional formulations, when repeated unchanged in novel situations, take on different—sometimes radically different—meanings. Instead of protecting or transmitting the faith delivered once for all to the saints, they may in fact betray it. Change in the interpretation and doctrinal formulation of scriptural truth is therefore demanded by unswerving faithfulness to that truth.[14]

4. There are some who carry this principle to such an extreme as to overlook the elements of continuity and cumulativeness in doctrinal development. However, among those who have studied the problem, even those who are regarded by some as radicals are well aware of the importance of these elements.[15] Doctrinal

[14] These formulations are in part suggested by P. Tillich's "principle of correlation" which, when looked at as a descriptive historical generalization, seems to me to summarize effectively the view of the development of doctrine held even by many Protestants who object strenuously to Tillich's methodological use of the principle in constructing a systematic theology. Cf. his *Systematic Theology*, I (Chicago, 1951ff.), pp. 3-68.

[15] Cf., for example, G. Ebeling, "Tradition," in *RGG* VI, pp. 976-84. It should be noted that the principle laid down in this paragraph that scripture must be read in the light of how it has been understood by the entire community of believers, past and present, actually implies (even

formulation does not, cannot and should not proceed in a wholly episodic, atomistic and discontinuous fashion. Each generation must read scripture afresh, but it necessarily does this in partial dependence on its predecessors, even when (or, perhaps, particularly when) this dependence is unconscious or takes the form of reaction against the previous generation. It is therefore of utmost importance that the Church of today seek to correct its one-sidedness, partiality and distortions by studying and learning how our forefathers in the faith through the whole of history have understood the Gospel. To the extent that this is done, there is a certain progressive enrichment and enlargement of the Church's doctrinal formulations and interpretations of revelation. At the same time this development must be regarded not as analogous to organic growth or unfolding in which later stages are contained in and build upon the earlier, but rather as similar to the much weaker type of "progress" in comprehension. This comes from viewing and responding to one and the same object from different perspectives and circumstances.

5. In the context of this kind of historical situationalism, the bible can no longer be viewed as the sole "objective" source of doctrine (the believing community of interpreters in which the Holy Spirit works is, so to speak, the "subjective" source). Most Protestant theologians still use the language of the "sole source"; in a sense they do so quite rightly because, like the Reformers, they strongly repudiate the notion that tradition is a supplemen-

---

though this is not always recognized) a very strong view of the indispensability of doctrinal traditions for the *theological* reading of scripture —i.e., for its application to the present situation. Possibly it is not necessary for the biblical exegete to know the later history of Christian thought in order to determine the original "explicit" historical sense, but an understanding of the contemporary "implications" (i.e., that Word of God for today which is "implicit" in the bible) depends overwhelmingly on an awareness of how the Word has been heard in past situations. Another way of emphasizing the importance of tradition in this context of thought is to point out that the present situation of the community of faith, in terms of which it listens to the Word, is itself largely determined by past doctrinal traditions. These, therefore, are inevitably sources of the Church's continuing activity of doctrinal formulation, though not all in the sense of providing supplementary information about the contents of the deposit of faith.

tary channel—more or less closely united to scripture—of information about revelation. Scripture remains for them "materially sufficient" in the most complete possible sense. Yet they also clearly recognize, even if this is not always reflected in their words, that in addition to scripture the historical situation is a kind of objective source of the Church's doctrine in the way previously indicated.

6. However, many contemporary Protestants maintain that this in no way diminishes the primacy of scripture. It remains for them the sole norm—the *norma normans non normata*—just as decisively as it was for Calvin and Luther. All the teachings of the Church must be constantly tested by scripture and thus kept open to review, revision or perhaps even repeal. This is true, not only because all doctrinal formulations are inevitably inadequate and may, in some cases, even be or become dangerously misleading (presumably some Catholic theologians would agree with this in substance),[16] but also because the Church may be led to see in the light of new perspectives on revelation that it was actually in error, even in the original circumstances, in making this or that dogmatic decision. Because this must be granted as possible at least in principle, the Church cannot formally declare its dogmas to be infallible.

However, the fact that there is something like a consensus among the theological heirs of the Reformation on these six points does not mean that there is a similar agreement on their detailed implications or on how to answer the further questions that must inevitably be raised.

In the first place, there is little clarity on the immense possibilities of doctrinal development opened up by this approach. Once one adopts the view that the Church must respond creatively in its teaching and practice to new circumstances, then any development which cannot be shown on responsible exegetical grounds to be at variance with the Gospel must be regarded, as far as the scriptural principle goes, as at least possibly legiti-

---

[16] G. Lindbeck, "Reform and Infallibility," in *Cross Currents* 11 (1961), pp. 345ff.

mate. The theological case for its legitimacy is further strengthened to the degree that it can be represented as positively in
harmony with, inspired by or implicit in the scriptural witness.
This is the kind of argument Protestants can advance for certain
developments, such as infant baptism,[17] which many of their
Churches in fact accept as highly authoritative. But essentially
the same kind of argument can be made for the possible legitimacy (not the dogmatization) of the more "evangelical" ver-
sions of certain Catholic teachings, including even the Marian
ones[18] which Protestants generally wish to exclude. Such rigidity
would seem to be inconsistent with the contemporary historical
view that development necessarily proceeds beyond scripture;
however, it should also be noted that a more open attitude is
often displayed toward Eastern Orthodox Mariological developments by Protestant theologians who, when they address themselves to Rome, continue to exhibit the traditional polemic re-
flexes. The recognition is gradually spreading that God may
grant further insights into his truth far beyond anything which
the Reformers envisioned, and that some thousands of years from
now, if human history still continues, the Church may be firmly
convinced that there are implicit in the original deposit of faith
theologoumena beyond our present imaginings.

It should be observed that this greater openness to development
finds some support in the willingness of the Reformers, particularly the Lutheran ones, to acknowledge the legitimacy of post-
apostolic traditions as long as they are not in contradiction to
scripture. To be sure, since they did not regard developments as
responses to the revelation to which scripture gives witness, they
were unable to see that certain traditions originating in post-
apostolic times might be of great doctrinal importance. Instead,
they indiscriminately classified all such developments as *adia-*

---

[17] In citing infant baptism as a post-apostolic development, I of course
do not mean to deny the (historically unverifiable) possibility that it
may occasionally have been practiced in the New Testament period; I
simply point out that it did not become a widespread practice, even for
the children of Christian parents, until very much later.

[18] I have in mind such presentations as those of K. Rahner, *Schriften*
I, pp. 223-52.

phora, as matters of indifference.[19] The contemporary historical approach is leading to a revision of this attitude, as is evident, for example, in the higher theological significance now given to the historic episcopacy even by those who think of it as a post-apostolic development.[20]

We have been speaking of legitimate developments and have indicated in passing that some, though not all, of these can be dogmatically defined—i.e., made into tests of orthodoxy and heresy. This brings us to a second area of disagreement. Many Protestant theologians doubt that there can be dogmatic developments in this sense, or at least are uncertain as to the conditions under which these can properly occur. We see this reflected in the fact that the phrase "dogmatic statements" is often used as an equivalent for "statements contained within a dogmatic system"—i.e., a systematic theology—[21] which presumably are often no more than *theologoumena.* This problem is simply the most acute form of what we have suggested is the major Protestant difficulty with development. How can post-biblical creeds and confessions (or, for that matter, decisions such as those against slavery or against nazism) become genuinely binding in the sense of determining the visible limits of Church fellowship without compromising the supreme authority of scripture?

A Protestant answer is that this becomes possible whenever (a) it is necessary to choose between alternatives on some matter which is vital to the faith; (b) only one of these is compatible with the scriptural witness. To cite a familiar illustration, these conditions were fulfilled at the time of the Arian controversies when it was necessary for the Church to make a decision on an issue which had never before been sharply and inescapably posed —namely, "Is Christ *fully* God?" or, soteriologically formulated, "Does our salvation depend wholly on the one God, or partly on a creature?" It may be granted to the historians that it is

---

[19] Cf. the comment on this in reference to liturgy by L. Jordahl, "The Adiophora Syndrome," in *Una Sancta* 22 (1965), pp. 76-80.

[20] E. Schlink, *Der kommende Christus und die kirchlichen Traditionen* (Göttingen, 1961), pp. 160-95.

[21] E. Pannenberg, *op. cit.* (footnote 8 *supra*), pp. 339-61.

quite impossible to deduce the *homoousion* from scripture; however, given the way in which the question was formulated, this provided the only possible concretely available answer which was consonant with scripture. Therefore, the decision in its favor was, so to speak, demanded by the bible, even though the words in which it was expressed were not. What thus distinguishes a dogmatizable development from a simply legitimate one is that the former is not only in harmony with scripture, but is, in addition, an objectively necessary defense against a vital threat to the integrity of the Gospel.[22]

From this perspective, the possibilities of dogmatic—in contrast to simply legitimate—development are much more severely restricted than in Catholic thought. The definitions of the immaculate conception and the assumption, to cite these examples once again, are excluded not only because it would be difficult to argue that they are necessary for the sake of the center of the Gospel, but also because they cannot be represented on objective exegetical grounds as the only ones among the available alternative views of Mary that are in harmony with scripture.[23] These developments may be theologically legitimate, but they are not dogmatizable.

These criteria for dogma are perhaps not often stated explicitly,[24] but they do articulate widespread Protestant attitudes. Those whose thinking proceeds along ecumenical lines insist that now, as in the early Church, it is important to recognize the legitimacy of a variety not only of theological formulations, but

[22] It should be noted that, in this view, a non-dogmatic development may have great authority in the Church, but it cannot be made the basis for declarations of heresy.

[23] It will be observed that the Orthodox view of what can and cannot be dogmatically defined is similar to this. Cf. J. Meyendorff, "Contemporary Orthodox Conception of the Church," in *Ecumenism and Vatican II*, edited by C. O'Neill (Milwaukee, 1964), pp. 28ff.

[24] However, it is not entirely absent. Cf. E. Kinder, "Dogmatik u. Dogma," in *Dogma und Denkstrukturen*, edited by W. Joest and W. Pannenberg (Göttingen, 1963), pp. 22-23: "Immer liegt dem Dogma eine Glaubensentscheidung in bezug auf solche Punkte der christilichen Gottes—und Heilsbotschaft zugrunde, die Kirche in ihrem Sein, Leben und Handeln als enscheidend und unabdingbar erfahren hat, mit denen ihr "Esse" als Kirche steht und fällt."

of creedal and confessional formulations as well. The unity of the Church requires the mutual recognition of these different formulations insofar as they are compatible with each other.[25] This implies, of course, that the Church should refrain as much as possible from dogmatizing developments (i.e., imposing uniformity). There also is the recognition that sometimes the Church must make dogmatic decisions distinguishing between heterodoxy and orthodoxy—the Barmen declarations are the most vivid recent example. Finally, there is the universal conviction, which we have already mentioned, that these decisions cannot be formally declared by the Church to be infallible, irreformable or irreversible.

This last point needs amplification, particularly, perhaps, for Catholic readers. It does not imply that the Church should be in a constant state of turmoil and uncertainty regarding its dogmas. Many contemporary Protestants are as "morally certain" as were the Reformers of the basic correctness of the decisions in the early centuries regarding the Trinity and christology and of those in the 16th century regarding justification and the *sola scriptura*. To take a particular example, they cannot imagine circumstances in which the *homoousion* would appear as the non-scriptural choice over against the Arians, even though they may think that this particular word, as well as its associated conceptuality, is now of doubtful intelligibility and relevance and that it needs to be explained extensively in order to correct the misleading connotations it has acquired. However, they would add that the Church cannot transpose its moral certainty regarding this or that teaching into a juridical and dogmatic declaration of infallibility. This is to do much more than insist that the acceptance (or non-rejection) of Nicaea is a condition for Church fellowship. It is rather to say that the Church is empowered to exempt from God's eschatological judgment any of its teachings of

---

[25] E. Schlink, *op. cit.* (footnote 18 *supra*), pp. 24-79. This essay, entitled "Die Struktur der dogmatischen Aussage als ökumenischen Problem", has proved fundamental for recent Roman Catholic and Protestant discussions of the relationship between diversity in doctrinal formulations and unity in faith.

which it is firmly convinced. It is to deny that there is no objective guarantee regarding the rightness of any of the human aspects of the Church; it is to deny that there is an element of risk involved in faith and therefore also in every effort to be faithful and obedient to God's Word. The *sola scriptura,* as well as the eschatological lordship of the coming Christ to which it bears witness, forbids the formal attribution of irreversibility to even the most necessary dogmatic developments.

There is much more that could be said about this topic. For example, the magisterial infallibility of the Church, which Protestants deny, is ultimately related to its "ontological" indefectibility, which they affirm. Approached from this latter angle, it might perhaps be possible, without attenuating the scriptural principle, to approach something like the Orthodox, even if not the Roman Catholic, understanding of infallibility.

In conclusion, we must return to our starting point and say something of what is really the major difficulty with maintaining the *sola scriptura* in the present situation. We have seen that it is possible to give an effective place to post-biblical developments while still insisting on a distinctively Reformation understanding of that principle. Some of what we have said goes substantially beyond the usual Protestant treatments, but it is not in disagreement with most of them. Yet this theory of post-biblical doctrinal development, if we may call it that, is of secondary importance because the vital threat to the *sola scriptura* comes from another quarter.

This threat comes, as we have said, from the historical studies which have shown the extent and variety of doctrinal development within the New Testament itself. From this the leading Protestant exegete, E. Käsemann, concludes, in a statement which has become famous: "The New Testament canon is not the ground of the unity of the Church but rather of the diversity of the confessions." [26] The question he raises is whether there is such an irreducible contrariety of theologies in the New Testa-

---

[26] E. Käsemann, *Exegetische Versuche und Besinnungen* I (Göttingen, 1960), p. 221. The essay from which this is taken has been translated in *Essays on New Testament Themes* (London, 1964), pp. 95-107.

ment that it is impossible to find by exegetical methods a single hermeneutical norm internal to it whereby the whole should be interpreted. If so, the Reformation principle that the bible is its own interpreter must be abandoned, and the theologically significant interpretation of the bible comes to depend ultimately on some external norm derived either from the subjectivity of the faith response (as the sectarian enthusiasts have always held) or on the doctrinal traditions and decisions of the Church, as Roman Catholics would say.

Käsemann, as well as other exegetes who argue in this way, tend to appeal to a "canon within the canon". Interestingly enough, this happens to correspond rather closely to what the Reformation considered the clearer parts of scripture in terms of which the more obscure should be understood—namely, the Christ-event, especially as interpreted by St. Paul.[27] This choice is not wholly subjective and arbitrary because Paul's writings are chronologically the earliest and theologically without rival (which is not at all to minimize the other parts of the New Testament). Thus these Protestant critics are in substantial agreement with the Reformers that Scripture is self-interpreting and that it identifies its own hermeneutical center.[28] The point at which they fundamentally disagree is their contention that other New Testament theologies (e.g., the "early Catholicism" of Luke-Acts and the pastoral epistles) are so basically incompatible with this center that they cannot be accorded any genuine canonical authority whatsoever without abandoning essential aspects of the Pauline position (and vice versa).[29]

By and large, this thesis of historically demonstrable incompatibility does not seem to be making much headway except in

---

[27] *Ibid.*, pp. 224ff.; Eng. tr., pp. 54ff. A summary of this discussion with references to the relevant literature is in J. Elliott, "The New Testament Is Catholic: A Reevaluation of the 'Sola Scriptura'," in *Una Sancta* 23 (1966), pp. 3-18.

[28] G. Ebeling, *op. cit.* (footnote 1 *supra*), p. 124: "Und deswegen wird durch Käsemanns These m. E. durchaus nicht das recht verstandene reformatorische Kanonsverständnis kritisch getroffen."

[29] H. Küng, *Strukturen der Kirche* (Freiburg, 1962), pp. 141ff.; Eng. tr.: *Structures of the Church* (New York, 1964), pp. 148ff. In this work Küng discusses these problems from a Catholic perspective.

German-speaking lands. While it is certainly true, as recent historical studies have shown, that one cannot systematically harmonize the various New Testament theologies as earlier generations sought to do, it is also *prima facie* impossible to prove their inconsistency. They admittedly represent radically different responses to the Gospel from within radically different situations and at times they may even have been in concrete conflict, but this is quite different from saying that they are incompatible. Paul's eschatology is both realized and futuristic while John's is almost entirely realized, but such differences in emphasis, even when radical, do not prove a contradiction by the canons either of logic or of everyday life. The younger English-speaking theologians are particularly sensitive to this point, for they have been alerted by the influence of Anglo-Saxon linguistic-analytic philosophy to the extreme difficulty of demonstrating consistency or inconsistency even in logical theory, and the problem becomes immensely greater when dealing with "ordinary" or "religious" sets of statements.

This insight frees the theologian, not to seek a single system of doctrine in scripture, but to view the New Testament in terms somewhat similar to those we have used in dealing with later centuries. All the developments in the canonical literature are authoritative, but only insofar as the primacy of hermeneutical center is maintained. John cannot be emphasized in such a way as to minimize the cosmic and futuristic messianism of Paul (which in turn is an interpretation of the earliest strata of the synoptic tradition and of the Old Testament itself). Nor can we so stress the early Catholic hierarchical ordering of the Church as to forget that, from a Pauline perspective, this would perform its proper function only in serving the charismatic freedom and equality of the members of the Spirit-filled community. When this approach is adopted, the initially disruptive emphasis on theological diversity becomes constructive. For example, the diversity in the early Church then becomes a normative paradigm for the inclusiveness and often tension-filled variety, combined with mutual recognition and fellowship, which should characterize the universal Church.

Thus, instead of marking the end of the *sola scriptura,* the present hermeneutical debates may perhaps produce a deeper and more ecumenical understanding that the biblical witness should operate as that supreme norm of all later developments which God uses to keep his Church faithful to the Lord who has come and is coming again.

PART III
DO-C DOCUMENTATION
CONCILIUM

Office of the Executive Secretary
Nijmegen, Netherlands

Walter Kasper/*Münster, W. Germany*

The Relationship between Gospel and Dogma: An Historical Approach

W
ith Vatican Council II the Catholic Church inaugurated dialogue with those of another faith or no faith. The Catholic notion of dogma seems to create a serious obstacle to the pursuit of this dialogue.[1] For many people today dogma appears to express a lack of liberty which contradicts man's dignity; for them dogma is loaded with historical memories of inquisition, condemnation, exile, persecution, burning and violence done to the human conscience. It is not merely one or other particular dogma, but the very fact that there is such a thing as dogma that constitutes for many an almost insuperable barrier to their access to the Gospel. To them there appears to exist a vast gulf between the Good News of the freedom of the children of God and dogma.

In order to find an answer to these questions about the relationship between Gospel and dogma it might be useful to approach the problem in the light of history. Here two points may be mentioned: (1) even within Catholic theology no solution

[1] In regard to this question, cf. K. Rahner, "Was ist eine dogmatische Aussage?" in *Schriften zur Theologie* V (Einsiedeln, 1962), pp. 54-81; W. Kasper, *Dogma unter dem Wort Gottes* (Mainz, 1965); *idem,* "Evangelium und Dogma," in *Catholica* 19 (1965), pp. 199-209; K. Rahner and K. Lehmann, "Kerygma und Dogma," in *Mysterium Salutis.* Grundrisz heilsgeschichtlicher Dogmatik, I (Einsiedeln, 1965), pp. 622-703; V. Schurr, "Kerygma and Dogma," in *Concilium* 3: *The Pastoral Mission of the Church* (1965), pp. 145-52.

153

has yet been found which is satisfactory and covers every aspect; this lack of clarity has given rise to many misunderstandings; (2) the older tradition of the Church contained a number of aspects which have vanished from the average man's present-day understanding of dogma but which may be helpful in our pastoral and theological situation. In this connection the link between Gospel and dogma as seen in scripture is of primary importance.

I

THE LIVING GOSPEL AND OBLIGATORY DOGMA
AS SEEN IN SCRIPTURE

The Gospel is a key concept of the New Testament.[2] According to Mark, Jesus preached the Gospel in these terms: "The time is fulfilled, and the kingdom of God is at hand" (1, 15). "Gospel" does not here mean an abstract doctrine but an event in which, with the coming of Jesus, the time is fulfilled, and in which, through his words and his deeds, the kingdom of God has become present. This Gospel asks man not merely to hold a doctrine as true but to make an unconditional decision involving his whole being: "Be converted and believe in the glad tidings!" The word of the Gospel is an active word; it does what it says and it gives what it promises. However, it operates in a way which stands open only to faith. From the purely human point of view, Jesus' proclamation failed on the cross; therefore, the promise of the Gospel lies beyond instant fulfillment. The Gospel, first of all, opens up the hope of total fulfillment in the future. It is an historical concept that points to the future, a prophetic power which, instead of closing the future, opens it up. It is always a living Gospel.

The word "Gospel" in the Church's history has always func-

[2] G. Friedrich, "Euaggelízomai, euaggélion," in *Theol. Wörterb. z. N.T.* II, pp. 705-35; P. Bläser, "Evangelium," in *Handbuch theol. Grundbegriffe* I, pp. 355-63; F. Mussner, "Evangelium und Mitte des Evangeliums," in *Gott in Welt.* Festgabe für K. Rahner, I (Freiburg im Br., 1964), pp. 492-514.

tioned as dynamite, breaking through all kinds of institutional and doctrinal petrifaction. There is no need to think in this connection of heretical and schismatic movements which sought to appeal to the word of the Gospel; one may also think of Francis of Assisi who asked Innocent III to be allowed to live according to the Gospel and so to bring about a reform of the Church from within.

Nevertheless, it would be wrong to see in the concept of "Gospel" a tendency which on principle is anti-institutional and anti-dogmatic. In the message of the living Gospel scripture is connected with fixed confessional formulae.[3] The clearest instance of this is 1 Corinthians 15, 3-5 where Paul designates a fixed confessional formula, taken from tradition, as "gospel". Elsewhere in the New Testament similar formulae can be found, such as those that arose out of baptism, the celebration of the eucharist, the controversies with false teachers or exorcisms (Rom. 1, 3; 10, 9; Phil. 2, 6ff.; Col. 1, 15ff.; 1 Tim. 3, 16, and other texts). Similarly we also find in the New Testament sentences of sacred law;[4] the anathema has a fixed place in the liturgy of the Lord's supper (1 Cor. 16, 22).[5] There are even clear indications for the organization of the community (Mt. 18).[6]

This disposes of a vital prejudice of liberal theology which opposes spirit to law and Gospel to dogma.[7] According to R. Bultmann, the connection between truth and law, which is a

---

[3] C. H. Dodd, *The Apostolic Preaching and Its Developments* (London, 1944); O. Cullmann, *Die ersten christlichen Glaubensbekenntnisse*. Theol. Studien, 15 (Zollikon-Zürich, [2]1949); J. R. Geiselmann, *Jesus der Christus. Die Urform des apostolischen Kerygmas als Norm unserer Verkündigung und Theologie von Jesus Christus* (Stuttgart, 1951); H. Schlier, "Kerygma und Sophia. Zur neutestamentlichen Grundlegung des Dogmas," in *Die Zeit der Kirche* (Freiburg im Br., 1958), pp. 206-32.

[4] E. Käsemann, "Sätze heiligen Rechts im Neuen Testament," in *Exegetische Versuche und Besinnungen* II (Göttingen, 1964), pp. 69-82.

[5] G. Bornkamm, "Das Anathema in der urchristlichen Abendmahlsliturgie," in *Das ende des Gesetzes. Gesammelte Aufsätze* I (Munich, 1963), pp. 123-32.

[6] W. Trilling, *Das wahre Israel. Studien zur Theologie des Matthäus-Evangeliums. Studien zum AT und NT*, 10 (Munich, [3]1964), pp. 106-23.

[7] E. Käsemann, *op. cit.*, pp. 80f.

constitutive element of dogma, was already prepared in the New Testament.[8]

However, these statements do not allow us to draw hasty and too far-reaching conclusions. The confessional formulae of the New Testament are not simply dogmas in the present sense. Most of them have no universal validity but only one that is more or less local; they are never taken as doctrinal laws but remain linked to the actual confessional situation, and their accentuation and further development depend on the changing situations. There is therefore a multiplicity of such confessions, rich in tensions, within the one New Testament, the unity of which is not a static and mechanical uniformity but a dynamic and historical value. Gospel and scripture are therefore not simply identical and the individual confessional formulae simply cannot be situated on the same level as the Gospel. The Gospel is always wider and more comprehensive than the individual formulae of the faith.

Behind this situation, which frequently confuses the modern onlooker, stands the specifically New Testament concept of truth.[9] In the sense of scripture, that is true which proves itself to be true, which shows itself in history to be what it asserts to be. Truth is not so much the recognized here-and-now correspondence between subject and object, but rather the identity of both, becoming clear as such in the future. Truth is always at the same time faithfulness and is essentially linked with the promise. Truth, therefore, can never be adequately contained in sentences; it will constantly break through the limits of any statement and always consist in something more, an overflowing of the promise beyond the present fulfillment. In the sense of

[8] R. Bultmann, "Alétheia," in *Theol. Wörterb. z. N.T.* I, p. 245.
[9] A. Schletter, *Der Glaube im Neuen Testament* ([5]1963), pp. 551-61; H. von Soden, "Was ist Wahrheit?" in *Urchristentum und Geschichte* (Tübingen, 1951), pp. 1-24; R. Bultmann, "Untersuchungen zum Johannesevangelium," in *Zeitschr. f. neutest. W.* 27 (1928), pp. 113-63; G. Quell, G. Kittel and R. Bultmann, "Alétheia," in *Theol. Wörterb. z. N.T.* I, pp. 233-51; J. de la Potterie, "De sensu vocis 'emeth' in Vetere Testamento," in *Verbum Domini* 27 (1949), pp. 336-54; 28 (1950), pp. 29-42; O. Loretz, *Die Wahrheit der Bibel* (Freiburg im Br., 1964); W. Kasper, *Dogma unter dem Wort Gottes* (Mainz, 1965), pp. 65-98.

scripture, truth has always an element of surprise, of something new, of something that goes beyond. The Spirit who reminds us of the truth of Christ which happened in the past is at the same time the Spirit of prophecy who leads us into the truth and announces the future (Jn. 16, 13). The truth of the formulae of faith is therefore always at the same time decisive and provisional; it is always imperfect (1 Cor. 13, 9. 12) because eschatologically it will only be manifest in the end. Heresy is possible in the New Testament not merely through the denial of already fixed formulae of faith, but also through the rigid clinging to these formulae in a new confessional situation where they lead to misunderstanding, become unsatisfactory and must therefore be understood afresh.[10]

This dynamic and historical aspect of the truth of the Gospel [11] was later forgotten in large measure. Thus dogma often became a fixed doctrinal sentence which seemed to lack totally that future dimension essential to the truth of the Gospel. In spite of this the older tradition of the Church maintained this connection of dogma with the living faith of the Church and thus preserved essential aspects of the biblical message.

II

DOGMA AND THE LIVING FAITH
ACCORDING TO THEOLOGICAL TRADITION

The historian of the relationship between Gospel and dogma must not stare himself blind on these two concepts but should rather study the underlying reality they imply. The notion of "Gospel" has played a curiously small part in the Church's tradition; the notion of "dogma" only became a technical term in modern times, and in its present meaning only dates from the end

[10] H. Koester, "Häretiker im Urchristentum als theologisches Problem," in Zeit und Geschichte. Festschrift für R. Bultmann (Tübingen, 1964), pp. 61-76.
[11] V. Berning, P. Neuenzeit and H. R. Schlette, Geschichtlichkeit und Offenbarungswahrheit (Munich, 1964).

of the 18th century.[12] This history of the words is not accidental: behind it lies an important change in the understanding of what we today call "dogma". The older tradition of the Church knows of other notions that reveal other aspects.

The earliest formulae of faith were understood as confessions (doxologies)[13] that were part of the baptismal and eucharistic liturgy. They were not primarily concerned with doctrinal statements, but with a personal, worshiping and praising confession of God and the deeds of his salvation. In this situation the dogma was not an independent doctrinal formula but rather pointed beyond itself to God and expressed an offering of praise and thanksgiving.

This dynamic concept of dogma was still known by the great theologians of the Middle Ages who, in general agreement, defined it as follows: "The article [of faith] is a perception of divine truth, tending towards this truth" (*articulus est perceptio divinae veritatis tendens in ipsam*).[14] The article of faith, therefore, is a real perception, and not a mere symbol or code formula; it is a perception which points beyond itself toward the greater mystery of God himself (DS 806).

The development from confession to doctrinal formulation started at an early date. Unlike the Nicene-Constantinopolitan Creed, that of Chalcedon was not incorporated in the liturgy.[15] The dogma then became the correct interpretation of the confession which was taken for granted. It is no longer a matter of opposing faith to unbelief but rather of orthodoxy to heterodoxy, and it now sought to build up the confession of faith. Thus the dogma became the rule of faith (*regula fidei, regula veritatis, canon veritatis*).

Here we meet with a second notion which is instructive for the understanding of dogma in the ancient Church. At that time

---

[12] Cf. *infra*, footnotes 19 and 20.

[13] E. Schlink, "Die Struktur der dogmatischen Aussage als ökumenisches Problem," in *Kerygma und Dogma* 3 (1957), pp. 251-306.

[14] J. M. Parent, "La notion de dogme au XIIIe siècle," in *Etude d'histoire litt. et doctr. du XIIIe siècle* (Paris, 1932), pp. 141-63.

[15] E. Schlink, *op. cit.*, pp. 265f.

the notion of "rule of faith" did not have the meaning which we understand today. It did not mean a rule which the Church's magisterium lays down for the faith (objective genitive) but the rule which is the faith itself (subjective genitive). The decisive element was not a formal juridical authority but rather the authority inherent in the contents of the faith itself.[16] It was not the formula as such that was considered infallible, but the Spirit who testified to himself in that formula.[17] This view could well become prevalent again today since the Church's proclamation can only rouse the faith when it brings the contents of the faith to light in such a way that it persuades man and moves him from within. Modern man is not impressed by the formal authority of the Church but only by the contents of the Church's message.

This virtue of dogma to transform from within is also seen in another concept which in some way corresponds in medieval theology to our "dogma": the article of faith (*articulus fidei*).[18] There were three elements that were considered essential to this concept: (1) it must be directly and formally contained in the revelation; (2) it must have in view man's ultimate goal, the beatific vision; (3) it must belong to the creed (which, since the Fourth Lateran Council, could also be understood in a broader sense).

For this discussion the second point is particularly interesting. According to the prevalent view in that period of the Middle Ages, a dogma does not merely state an objective truth in itself but must always have some relevance for human existence and man's self-awareness. A dogma's value for life decides the meas-

[16] D. van den Eynde, *Les normes de l'enseignement chrétien dans la littérature patristique des trois premiers siècles* (Gembloux, 1933), pp. 281-313; Y. Congar, *Die Tradition und die Traditionen* I (Mainz, 1965), pp. 43-48; B. Häggelund, "Die Bedeutung der 'regula fidei' als Grundlage theologischer Aussagen," in *Studia theologica* 12 (1958), pp. 1-44.

[17] *L'infaillibilité de l'Eglise.* Journées œcuméniques de Chevetogne, 25-29 septembre, 1961 (Chevetogne, 1963).

[18] J. M. Parent, *op. cit.;* A. Lang, "Die Gliederung und Reichweite des Glaubens nach Thomas von Aquin und den Thomisten," in *Divus Thomas* 20 (1942), pp. 207-36, 335-46; 21 (1943), pp. 79-97; L. Hödl, "Articulus fidei. Eine begriffsgeschichtliche Arbeit," in *Einsicht und Glaube.* Festschrift f. G. Söhngen (Freiburg im Br., 1962), pp. 358-76.

ure and the reason for its being a dogma at all. This important aspect also found expression in Vatican Council I which held that the truths of faith must be interpreted in the light of their relation to the ultimate end of man (DS 3016). Dogmas must serve to enlighten man's existence and not merely serve abstract speculation.

However, a dogma has as its object not merely particular individuals but rather the whole Church as the communion of the faithful. It therefore has a function which is both social and ecclesial. This is shown in two further concepts that run parallel to our notion of dogma today—namely, faith and heresy (*fides* and *haeresis*).[19] The concept of faith, as understood in the Middle Ages, surpasses our present notion in two ways: (1) it embraces not only the content of the faith (*fides quae*) but also the subjective attitude to the faith (*fides qua*); (2) it is not strictly limited to the revealed truths of faith but also comprises all that belongs to the attitude of a consistent faith in the Church. The content of the faith is therefore not detached in this concept from the living fulfillment and perception of the Church. Faith and the Church's life belong together.

This aspect is very important for the correct interpretation of dogma. It does not suffice to point to a bare text in Denzinger or to quote a papal encyclical. A dogma must also be understood in the light of its age, chronologically, intellectually and theologically. Since the definition of a dogma is not always immediately followed by the Church's interpretation of it, many dogmas after their proclamation often go through a complicated and frequently astonishing process of interpretation before their real meaning becomes clear. We can watch this process, for instance, between the Councils of Nicaea (325) and Constantinople I (381), or between the Council of Ephesus (431) and those of Chalcedon (451) and Constantinople II (553). We

[19] A. Lang, *op. cit.; idem,* "Der Bedeutungswandel der Begriffe 'fides' und 'haeresis' und die dogmatische Wertung der Konzilsentscheidungen von Vienne und Trient," in *Münch. Theol. Zeitschr.* 4 (1953), pp. 133-46.

ourselves have experienced this process in the passage from Vatican Council I to Vatican Council II.

On the other hand, we should not overlook the defectiveness of this medieval view; it too easily blurs the sharp contours of the obligatory character of statements by the magisterium and therefore does not always leave the necessary room for freedom to move within the Church. This sharp line of demarcation between formal dogma and simple ecclesiastical teaching was drawn by theology only in modern times when the present concept of dogma was formulated.

III

The Authoritative Character of Dogma in Post-Tridentine Theology

It is only in more modern theology that the concept of dogma[20] began to play a decisive role. The history of the concept in the patristic period and the Middle Ages has relatively little to say on this point. The formulae of faith of the old Councils were never called "dogmas"; this idea remained reserved for disciplinary decisions. (An exception must be made for the *Commonitorium* of Vincent of Lerins who died before 450 and the work of a contemporary of his, Gennadius, who died about 492.) Nor did it play a part worth mentioning during the whole medieval period.

Not until the 16th century was the concept introduced into theological language with a kind of "renaissance" of Vincent of Lerins. It was useful as a basis for the anti-Reformation controversies; over against the "new dogma" of the Reformers one

---

[20] A. Deneffe, "Dogma: Wort und Begriff," in *Scholastik* 6 (1931), pp. 381-400, 505-38; G. Kittel, "Dogma," in *Theol. Wörterb. z. N.T.* II, pp. 233-35; J. Ranft, "Dogma, I," in *Reallex. f. Ant. u. Chr.* III, pp. 1257-60; E. Fascher, "Dogma, II," *ibid.* IV, pp. 1-24; J. R. Geiselmann, "Dogma," in *Handbuch theol. Grundbegriffe* I, pp. 225-30; M. Elze, "Der Begriff des Dogmas in der Alten Kirche," in *Zeitschr. f. Theol. Kirche* 61 (1964), pp. 421-38; W. Kasper, *op. cit.*, pp. 28-38.

could, with Vincent of Lerins, appeal to the "universal and ancient faith" (*universalis ac vetusta fides*) of the Church. Because of this origin the notion of dogma had a certain denominational slant, but it also could be useful interdenominationally. As far as we know, it was used for the first time in its present connotation by F. Veronius, S.J. (1575-1649), from whom it was borrowed by P. N. Chrismann, O.F.M. (1751-1810).[21] Both men strove to free themselves from the sterile theology of the controversies, to keep ecclesiastical teaching and mere theological opinion apart, and thus to limit the interdenominational dialogue to formal ecclesiastical doctrine. Therefore, we have in principle the present notion of dogma which regards as revealed truth that which is declared by the Church either as part of the universal teaching or through a solemn doctrinal judgment. In this sense dogma contains two elements: divine revelation and the Church's proposing of it.

Apart from this "confessional" (denominational) motive, there is another, rooted in the development of cultural history, which is perhaps even more decisive for the modern notion of dogma.[22] The modern age is marked by a radical break with tradition. For almost 1,500 years the Church had lived in reasonably obvious agreement with tradition, until the time when the Christian faith was queried in principle.

In reply, Vatican Council I was concerned with a basic self-assurance with regard to the faith. Over against a purely anthropocentric way of thinking, the Council placed the authority of God revealing himself (DS 3008) and it also stressed the obligatory authority and the irreducibility of the faith in this world. Over against the prevalent individualism it stressed the social and ecclesial bearing of the faith and the function of a magisterium which represented the community of the faithful and was authoritatively binding. These two aspects of this more recent

---

[21] P. Chrismann, *Regula fidei catholicae* (Kempten, 1792). On this point, cf. J. Beumer, "Die Regula fidei catholicae des Ph. N. Chrismann, O.F.M., und ihre Kritik durch J. Kleutgen, S.J.," in *Franziskanische Studien* 46 (1964), pp. 321-34.

[22] K. Rahner and K. Lehmann, *op. cit.*, pp. 651f.

notion of dogma should not be considered to be an exhaustive definition of the essence of dogma. Here they concern merely two fundamental and transcendental features of the essence of faith which were of particular importance in the situation of those days and which brought out an essential aspect of the Gospel. The Gospel is a call addressed to man, demanding a decision which is unconditional and embraces his whole being; it must therefore be proclaimed by the Church in a way that is dogmatically binding. But apart from the authoritative character of dogma, Vatican Council I also stressed its relativity. The Council made a clear distinction between the Gospel (the deposit of faith) and the ecclesiastical formulation of doctrine (the dogma).[23] The dogma is but an analogous, inadequate, human statement of divine truth (DS 3015f.).

The Church's tradition knows of a profusion of other aspects which found no place in the texts of Vatican Council I. Even today we do not yet have an adequate and comprehensive definition of what a dogma is. The unresolved questions arising from this situation have given rise to many misunderstandings both inside and outside the Church. The tragic dealings with modernism, so burdened through misunderstanding,[24] are but one proof of this fact. Apart from the hierarchical authoritative character of dogma, the anthropological meaning of the faith must be emphasized much more clearly.

IV

THE BINDING FORCE OF DOGMA AND THE
FREEDOM OF THE GOSPEL IN THE MODERN AGE

The Church has accepted dialogue with the modern world. It has abandoned many of those cramping limitations which accompanied the one-sided polemics and apologetics against "modern errors" and which drove the Church more and more into a

[23] J. R. Geiselmann, *op. cit.*, p. 229.
[24] E. Poulat, *Histoire, dogme et critique dans la crise moderniste* (Tournai, 1962); M. Blondel, *Geschichte und Dogma* (Mainz, 1963).

ghetto. The Church often defended the truth, but it no longer reached the concrete modern man with this truth, even though the glad tidings were destined for him. The process of receiving and adapting, which is an essential part of dogma, was considerably disrupted in modern times. Today the Church recognizes those positively human and often anonymously Christian concerns which operate in the modern world; often these concerns can also be observed where the Catholic understanding of dogma is rejected and resisted. Therefore, we must indicate the positive elements which this contemporary development contributes to the correct understanding of dogma.

In these days a dogmatic faith is often considered as unfree and unworthy of man. The mere faith in propositions was, for Kant, "groveling" and superstition.[25] From the early humanism of Erasmus up to the liberal theology of Adolf von Harnack, efforts were made to deliver modern man from the heavy and (for him) unbearable harness of philosophical concepts and so to restore to the faith its vitality and original intelligibility by taking it back to the simplicity of the Gospel.[26] However, the concrete execution of this basic project was often too rationalistic, resulting in a considerable curtailment of the Christian message. This the Church rightly rejected. Nevertheless, the basic issue remains valid and it is now being tackled by a pastoral-minded theology. This theology is concerned with man, his freedom and his dignity. Man, therefore, must not be presented with a faith that is overlaid with unintelligible formulae. The faith is not merely concerned with the authority of God but also with the humanity of man. The Church thus must show that the dogmas are not just formally obligatory, but that they are also meaningful in themselves, enlightening man in a human way and capable of fulfillment in faith with regard to the modern world.

---

[25] M. Blondel, *Die Religion innerhalb der Grenzen der bloszen Vernunft*, IV. Stück, 1. Teil; 2. Abschnitt (ed. W. Weischedel, IV), p. 835; *idem, Der Streit der Fakultäten*. 1. Abschnitt; 2. Kapitel (ed. W. Weischedel, VI), pp. 300ff.

[26] F. W. Kantzenbach, *Evangelium und Dogma*. Die Bewährung des theologischen Problems der Dogmengeschichte im Protestantismus (Stuttgart, 1959).

But this presents present-day preaching and theology with problems that have hardly been solved. These problems arise mainly from two causes:

1. The radical cultural revolution taking place today which affects our whole thinking at its very roots.[27] This does not mean that the Church's faith has become false, but that it has become largely incomprehensible in the shape it had until the present time. It must now be proclaimed and interpreted in such a way that it can provide an answer to the problems of modern man.

2. The pluralism which increasingly prevails in the world and in the Church. Up until now the history of dogma was really a piece of the cultural history of the West. It would be a novel kind of Judaism if the new nations were first asked to learn to think the Western way before they could become Christian.

Catholic theology can deepen its understanding of dogma not only in the dialogue with the modern world but also in the ecumenical dialogue with other Churches or beliefs. Here the difficulties lie not only in particular dogmas but in an often basic difference in the understanding of the overall nature and function of dogma. The Reformers preserved the dogmas of the ancient Church but, within their overall teaching on scripture and justification, they nevertheless gave them a new valuation. Their basic concern was to maintain the freedom of the Gospel over and above the Church.[28] If modern thought concerned itself with the freedom and dignity of man, here the issue was the freedom and primacy of the Word of God over the Church.

Although, in the Catholic view, this conception does not do full justice to the significance of the Church for salvation history, we nevertheless recognize here a legitimate preoccupation with something that is not sufficiently recognized in the average Catholic notion of dogma. Vatican Council II itself emphasizes that the Church is not superior to the Word of God but rather serves

[27] B. Welte, "Ein Vorschlag zur Methode der Theologie heute," in *Gott in Welt*. Festgabe f. K. Rahner, I (Freiburg im Br., 1964), pp. 271-86.

[28] J. Koopmans, *Das altkirchliche Dogma in der Reformation* (Munich, 1955); K. G. Steck, *Undogmatisches Christentum?* Theol. Exist., 48 (Munich, 1955); idem, *Kirche des Wortes oder Kirche des Lehramts?* (Zürich, 1962).

it.[29] Dogma is not merely a human, inadequate stammering in the face of God's mystery; it also involves the fact that the Church is always a Church of sinners. As a result a dogma may be true and yet be formulated in a manner which is too precipitate, overbearing, historically culpable, ambiguous, tempting or presumptuous; in certain circumstances it can maneuver man into a situation that is beyond him.[30]

A third factor contributing to the discussion within the Catholic Church is modern biblical exegesis.[31] In the past this was also hampered by a frequently sterile and purely apologetic approach. But here, too, the attitude has become more positive and open-minded since the encyclical *Divino afflante Spiritu* (1943), the recent statements of the biblical commission and the *Constitution on Divine Revelation* of Vatican Council II. The Council certainly emphasizes the interconnection of scripture, tradition and the magisterium,[32] but their interrelation is not the one-way process that it once was. It is no longer a question of interpreting scripture in the light of tradition and dogma; rather, the biblical scholar is now expected to make his contribution to the Church's judgment.[33] This means that the process may be inverted so that dogma must be understood in the light of scripture. The proper place, the right emphasis and the true perspective of later formulations of the faith must be found in the scriptural message.[34] And so the dialogue between dogmatic theology and exegesis shows once again that the Gospel, principally attested by scripture, is superior to dogma.

[29] *Dogmatic Constitution on Divine Revelation*, n. 10 (Glen Rock, N.J.: Paulist Press, 1966), p. 67.

[30] K. Rahner, "Was ist eine dogmatische Aussage?" *loc. cit.*, p. 58.

[31] *Exegese und Dogmatik*, ed. by H. Vorgrimler (Mainz, 1962); *Diskussion über die Bibel*, ed. by L. Klein (Mainz, ³1964); L. Scheffczyk, "Die Auslegung der Schrift als dogmatische Aufgabe," in *Münch. Theol. Zeitschr.* 15 (1964), pp. 190-204; W. Kasper, "Exegese—Dogmatik—Verkündigung," in *Diakonia* 1 (1966), pp. 3-12.

[32] *Dogmatic Constitution on Divine Revelation, op. cit.,* n. 9, pp. 66-67.

[33] *Ibid.,* n. 12, pp. 73-74.

[34] M. Löhrer, "Ueberlegungen zur Interpretation lehramtlicher Aussagen als Frage des ökumenischen Gesprächs," in *Gott in Welt*. Festschr. f. K. Rahner II (Freiburg im Br., 1964), pp. 499-523.

What then is a dogma? I do not intend to attempt a conclusive definition, for there is still too much that remains obscure. I will only summarize briefly the function of a dogma. A dogma is necessary for the unity and clarity of the faith. It is an aid to steer the act of faith into the right direction. For that reason a dogma expresses something final while at the same time remaining provisional. Its truth lies precisely in that it points beyond itself, in that it does not bar access to the Gospel, but shows itself capable of stimulating a live faith, hope and charity for the people of today. And this requires an interpretation of dogma which is dynamic, related to man and his problems, and spiritual and biblical in character.

M. C. Vanhengel, O.P./*Nijmegen, Netherlands*

J. Peters, O.C.D./*Nijmegen, Netherlands*

Theology and Theologies

W hen an international theological series like *Concilium* is represented at an international Congress, such as that held on the theology of Vatican Council II in Rome (September 26—October 1, 1966), it obviously will be mainly interested in assessing the international character of the seventy-two conferences and reports; apart from this, its theological representatives will want to check the program and general tendency of *Concilium* with whatever is produced at such a vast Congress. Therefore, given the necessary limitations and the impossibility of summarizing all the lectures and reports,[1] the reader should mainly be interested in these two points.

I

THE INTERNATIONAL CHARACTER OF THE CONGRESS

It would seem obvious that a group of 1,200 theologians who, within one week, have to listen to 72 conferences by professional colleagues, cannot possibly achieve a dialogue. One may also dispute the international character of such a meeting by pointing out that most of the participants were Italians and Spaniards, or that, even after subtracting this southern bloc, the Congress re-

[1] The Congress has made it known that all the conferences and reports will appear in book form. For those reports at which we could not be present, we are indebted to the much appreciated collaboration of Dr. R. Gibellini and Dr. G. Ruggieri.

mained nevertheless a Western European affair (although some Eastern European theologians were present), since the United States was in a minority and the new Christendom, such as that of Africa, was hardly represented. One might even point to the absence of such men as Küng, Haering and Metz and try to explain this in the light of rumors current in Rome. One might finally complain of the obviously too hasty organization or feel frustrated professionally at the manner in which the chairman of the Congress, E. Dhanis, proposed at the end some ten resolutions which were more or less the repetition in different words of the ten main subjects announced in the program. But all such observations only touch the surface of the Congress. We would prefer to concentrate on its reality because the usefulness of this Congress should not be looked for in outward results but rather in an inner shifting of mentality. There was no question of imposing a uniform Roman theology; there was plenty of room for a fruitful coexistence of various theologies within the one faith. This became clear not so much in the choice of subjects (a choice mainly determined by the main themes of Vatican Council II), but in the various ways in which these themes were approached and assessed. Some introductory speakers limited themselves scrupulously to an exegesis of the conciliar texts; others made use of the open space created by the Council and pursued the themes in the direction that the Council indicated. This latter tendency came to the fore particularly in the treatment of religious freedom, the Church's relationship and dialogue with the world, the value of other religions and of atheism and the treatment of ecumenism. It was also striking that the possibility of various theologies was explicitly mentioned in the pope's letter, of which every participant received a copy at the opening session, and in his long address at the closing session.[2] Only one

---

[2] Referring to the *Decree on Ecumenism* in the letter mentioned in the text, the pope said: "The advance in theological teaching really lies in this legitimate freedom. . . . It is therefore not surprising that one observes and explains certain aspects of a revealed mystery more accurately than another, so that one has to say that various theological formulations often complement each other rather than exclude each other." In his

theme was treated as if it were an exclusively Catholic concern (Mariology), but in the treatment of the other themes it became obvious every time we touched on a universal Christian problem, even if only in the form of a finely formulated question such as Congar put at the conference given by Colombo. Although the Congress did not achieve a genuine dialogue (except in the spacious foyer of the *domus pacis*), there was nevertheless a certain exchange between the various theologies. In order to clarify this we shall briefly look at the various themes with an eye on this exchange.

1. *The Church*

With the fact constantly in mind that the mystery of the Church is a prolongation of the incarnation, theologians tried on the one hand to see a continuity from the Church conceived as Christ's mystical body (Colombo, Tromp, Parente) to a closer definition of what the Church is in itself; on the other hand, there was constant emphasis on the dynamism of that reality which is the Church and its historicity (Congar): the Church as the growing historical manifestation of what salvation and world mean and ultimately are (Schillebeeckx). Referring to the synthesis of this dialectic, Ratzinger, when he spoke at a meeting of I-Doc, pointed to christology as preeminently the treatise of future theology.

2. *Collegiality*

The relationship between the pope and the episcopal college still appeared to be one of the sore spots of a theology that likes

---

closing address the pope said: "In such difficult matters which are, moreover, not accessible to ordinary experience—I refer to theological problems—a moderate difference of opinion is compatible with the unity of faith and faithful adhesion to the doctrines and norms of the magisterium" (*L'Osservatore Romano*, Oct. 20, 1966, p. 1).

to underline the necessary element of authority in the hierarchy. But in addition to the question about the apostolic succession with all its juridical implications and ecclesiastical complications, there were also timid suggestions of a more dynamic approach to apostolicity, which wanted to make the whole Church share in this apostolic succession since the whole Church has a mission in this world. This exchange caused one to expect in the future a broadening of the concept of succession and a more conscious questioning about its content (this succession is also necessary in prophecy and in the effective will toward redemption).

3. *Mariology*

The extremist approach to the problem of Mary as a purely Catholic concern only led to an opposite approach in the contribution made by Semmelroth.

4. *The Presence of the Lord*

This theme, to which particular attention was drawn after the Council by the encyclical *Mysterium fidei,* drew light from the fact that it was dealt with by various theologies. What had been put forward in recent times on this point as an "antithesis" to the "thesis" of transubstantiation was overtaken by Rahner's "synthesis" of the Lord's presence in the Church. However, he avoided using this category of "presence" as a kind of definition by way of a premise to his argument, although he managed to broaden it with great clarity in the sense of an anthropological reality. Within this new "breadth", argued phenomenologically, the Lord and his people are present to one another in the Church at different levels of intensity which cannot possibly be isolated from each other (Word, sacraments, eucharist). The eucharistic presence of the glorified Lord cannot be detached from the sphere of faith that contains this mutual relationship. It cannot be reduced to something physical. Precisely in a synthesis such as this one realizes how necessary are the results achieved by classical theology (Ciappi) and those achieved by an active liturgy (Jungmann).

5. *The Missionary Statute of the Church*

Although one still heard here the powerful voice of an essentialist theology which saw the missionary task of the Church in the Church's exclusive privilege and duty to proclaim salvation to all men, the voice of those who saw this salvation grow as an historical value in the non-Christian religions was more persuasive (Loffeld, Papali). The missiologist can hardly dispose of the suspicion of a spiritual colonialism by looking at it in a formally correct way, such as Masson who stated that the missionary inspiration of the Church springs from a *caritas fontalis* (a "source-charity"): it developed that it was not clear where this source was to be found. But even a subterranean source may bring about some fruitfulness.

6. *Salvation History*

The fallacy in speaking of a Roman or European or possibly American theology, or about a progressive or a conservative one, became obvious in Alszeghy's masterly treatment of salvation history as an historically growing reality. The content of salvation becomes constantly clearer and more explicit (reflective) when the theologian participates actively in this historical process and can penetrate to the transcendent element in this historicity. As Ratzinger indicated, transcending the phenomenological approach to human existence is a middle way between two extreme Christian viewpoints (Cullmann and Bultmann).

7. Scripture

The shades in the relationship between religious truth and revealed truth, between the absolute character of the Gospel and the historicity of the kerygma, presuppose shades in the questions about truth and values with which one approaches scripture and tradition (Benoît). Coppens dealt with the use of "truth" in the plural in the *Constitution on Divine Revelation*. To this Betti and Holstein added a persuasive plea for a post-conciliar theology of tradition.

8. Religious Freedom

On this point, too, voices were heard that were not yet joined in harmony. What kind of freedom are we talking about here? Is it the freedom of an institution (Jiménez)? Is it the freedom of man who, because of his human dignity, is also entitled to a free unfolding of his religious quality, or who, precisely in the unfolding of this quality, achieves freedom (John Courtney Murray), which in practice presupposes a broader approach than mere tolerance (Wright)? Or is it the privilege of a static truth which can only tolerate any deviation as a necessary evil? And so here, as in the previous topics, there was a pronounced demand for an anthropology and for passing beyond the purely internal problems of the Church.

9. The Dialogue between Church and World

Expectations ran high on this subject because of the presence of Msgr. McGrath, well known for his intervention in Schema 13, and such speakers as Congar, Daniélou and Chenu, as well as Max Thurian with his open-minded approach. The way the subject was dealt with, more than the practical conclusions, showed how much of value the world has already given to the Church. Therefore, to say the least, it was surprising that Karl

Barth, who happened to be in Rome at that time, tried to convince the "center" of the Church that it was going too far in this dialogue and that it would lose its relative autonomy by yielding to the temptation to which Protestantism had already succumbed: an equalization with the world.

10. *Ecumenism*

When we ask ourselves toward what kind of unity we are striving (Hamer), we are exposed to the temptation of thinking in terms of wishes which have nothing to do with a genuine theology. Hamer therefore pointed to two tendencies in this dialectic: a certain pluriformity of the Church which Protestant exegesis seems to suggest, and the one common task of bringing about peace and social and international justice and development. Thils gave a clear analysis of the Church as a community, and in this light showed that while no single institution fully realizes the community, yet each is rightly entitled to be called "Church". This was followed by Dejaifve's remarkable explanation of the legitimate variety of dogmatic formulations within the unity of faith.

The international character of this Congress lay principally in the varieties of approach. Of course it would be possible to arrange the report in another order of importance (e.g., 6, 8, 9, 1, 10, 5, 4, 2, 3) which might provide a better insight into what was presented and the coherence of the contents. However, it is more important to see how the Congress showed evidence of a theological reflection which is in touch with what the world is achieving in self-reflection and secular salvation.

II

WHAT DID THE CONGRESS OFFER IN CONNECTION
WITH CONCILIUM?

In his closing address the pope stressed, apart from the function of the magisterium, two necessary qualities of theology which *Concilium* has stressed from its very beginning: a spirit of service (*esprit de service*) and a spirit of communion (*esprit de communion*): to be of service to the Christian community and to the magisterium which serves the Church, while avoiding sensationalism, and to further a spirit of communion which is at the same time a spirit of community. This means contact and continuous exchange between the theologians, on the one hand, and the hierarchy, the bishops and faithful on the other. Moreover, it demands a mutual contact among the theologians who should show open-mindedness for each other's theology. Burdened by the heaviest office in the Church, the pope strongly appealed to the theologians to help him and his episcopal brethren to lighten this burden.

In the first volume of this series *Concilium* introduced itself with these words written by Rahner and Schillebeeckx: "It aims to offer information about new questions and new answers in *all* branches of theology, at regular intervals and *throughout the universal Church,* for those engaged in pastoral work, including qualified laymen who bear ecclesiastical responsibilities. It will do so in a factual, systematic manner, carefully selecting for special emphasis what is of outstanding importance to its particular group of readers. . . . It thereby aspires to be 'catholic' in the full sense of the word." [3]

We are not suggesting that *Concilium* has already fully realized what is contained in this declaration of intent. But the emphasis on this spirit of service and spirit of communion confirms it in its conviction that this formula was in the right direction.

[3] Cf. *Concilium* 1: *The Church and Mankind* (Glen Rock, N.J.: Paulist Press, 1965), p. 2.

BIOGRAPHICAL NOTES

PETER VAN LEEUWEN, O.F.M.: Born in 1913 in Leerdam, Netherlands, he was ordained in 1938. He studied at the Universities of Louvain and Nijmegen. He is a doctor of theology and teaches dogma at the Institut Théologique in Alverna, Netherlands. Among his publications should be mentioned *Het gemengde huwelijk* and *Pastoral-sociografisch onderzoek naar de huwelijken van katholieken en niet-katholieken in Nederland*. He contributes principally to the review *Oecumene* and to *Tijdschrift voor Theologie*.

LEO BAKKER, S.J.: Born in 1926 in Nijmegen, he was ordained in 1957. He studied at the Gregorian University in Rome, and gained his doctorate in theology in 1962. He teaches fundamental theology and the theology of spirituality at the Canisianum Institute, Maastricht (Netherlands). He has published many articles on problems of fundamental theology.

ANTON VÖGTLE: Born in 1910 in Vilsingen, Germany, he was ordained in 1936. He studied at the Universities of Freiburg-im-Breisgau and Tübingen, as well as at the Pontifical Biblical Institute in Rome. He gained his doctorate in theology in 1949 and has lectured on early Christian literature and exegesis at Trêve and at Freiburg-im-Breisgau. He has published numerous articles on biblical subjects and has written for the *Lexikon für Theologie und Kirche*.

JUAN ALFARO, S.J.: Born in 1914 in Carcastillo, Spain, he was ordained in 1944. He studied at the Pontifical Biblical Institute and at the Gregorian University. He gained his doctorate in dogmatic theology in 1950 and is presently professor of dogmatic theology at the Gregorian University and co-editor of *Sacramentum Mundi*. Among his publications is *Supernaturalitas fidei secundum S. Thomam* (1963). He contributes principally to the review *Gregorianum*.

GREGORY BAUM, O.S.A.: Born in 1923 in Berlin, he was ordained in 1954. He studied at the University of Fribourg (Switzerland) where he gained his doctorate with the thesis *That They May Be One*, in 1956, and is presently professor of theology at St. Michael's College in Canada. He is also consultant to the Secretariat for Christian Unity and editor of *The Ecumenist*. Among his publications is *Ecumenical Theology Today* (1964).

HANS URS VON BALTHASAR: Born in 1905 in Lucerne, he was ordained in 1936. He studied at the Universities of Vienna, Berlin and Zurich, and gained his doctorate in philosophy. Among his publications should be mentioned *Karl Barth, Darstellung u. Deutung* and *Science, Religion and Christianity*.

MARIE-DOMINIQUE CHENU, O.P.: Born in 1895 near Paris, he was ordained in 1918. He studied at the Angelicum in Rome and gained his doctorate in theology in 1920. He taught history of theology at the Saulchoir and then became a professor at the Sorbonne. Among his publications are *La théologie comme science au XIIIème siècle,* and *Pour une théologie du travail.* He contributes to the *Revue des sciences philosophiques et théologiques.*

HERBERT HAMMANS: Born in 1932 in Düren, Germany, he was ordained in 1959. He studied at the Universities of Innsbruck and Aix-la-Chapelle. He gained his doctorate in theology in 1961 with the thesis: *Die neueren katholischen Erklärungen der Dogmenentwicklung.*

GEORGE A. LINDBECK: Born in 1923 in Loyang, China, he is a member of the Lutheran Church. He gained his doctorate in philosophy in 1955 with the thesis: *Is Duns Scotus an Essentialist?* A teacher of the history of doctrine at Yale University Divinity School, he attended Vatican Council II as a Lutheran observer. He contributes to the *Journal of Ecumenical Studies,* and has written numerous articles on the Council, ecumenism, liturgical reform and religious liberty.

WALTER KASPER: Born in 1933 in Heidenheim, Germany, he was ordained in 1957. He studied at the Universities of Tübingen and Munich. He gained his doctorate in theology in 1961 and is professor of dogmatic theology at the University of Münster. Among his publications are *Das Absolute in der Geschichte* and *Philosophie und Theologie der Geschichte in der Spätphilosophie Schellings.*

International Publishers of CONCILIUM

ENGLISH EDITION
Paulist Press
Glen Rock, N. J., U.S.A.

Burns & Oates Ltd.
25 Ashley Place
London, S.W.1

DUTCH EDITION
Uitgeverij Paul Brand, N. V.
Hilversum, Netherlands

FRENCH EDITION
Maison Mame
Tours/Paris, France

GERMAN EDITION
Verlagsanstalt Benziger & Co., A.G.
Einsiedeln, Switzerland

Matthias Grunewald-Verlag
Mainz, W. Germany

SPANISH EDITION
Ediciones Guadarrama
Madrid, Spain

PORTUGUESE EDITION
Livraria Morais Editora, Ltda.
Lisbon, Portugal

ITALIAN EDITION
Editrice Queriniana
Brescia, Italy